No, Mom!

*Can I Tell My Aging Parents "No"
and Still Honor Them?*

Sherri Snider

Copyright © 2025

All Rights Reserved

No part of this book may be reproduced or transmitted in any form or by any means, electronic or mechanical, including photocopying, recording, or by any information storage and retrieval system without the written permission of the author, except where permitted by law.

Copyright registration number: TXu 2-462-584

ISBN: 979-8-9906176-2-9

To my husband, Karl

ACKNOWLEDGEMENTS

I am surrounded by women of astounding talent without whom I would be lost. Their individual giftedness has brought this book to fruition.

My editor, Bethany Spitzmiller (Spitzfire Editorial), has been with me through many projects, including my dissertation and my first book, a children's book titled, "Pippa Learns About Gran's Dementia." Her attention to detail and knowledge of grammar and sentence structure has put a professional touch on my writing. But, perhaps more importantly, she has gently guided me in how to better convey my thoughts in a way that is relatable to my readers. (That is not to say she hasn't learned something from my writing, such as the term "Katy, bar the door!") Through her expertise in editing, marketing, and web page developing, Bethany has worked diligently to bring me into this century—with moderate success (the fault is not that of the teacher, but rather of the pupil). Bethany has been a blessing and joy to me throughout her life, and I thank God for her.

The cover design of this book is the work of Ashley Hall (Ashley Hall Photography). All I had to do was describe my vision, and she brought it to life with a beautiful flair that only Ashley could achieve. I know of no one more creative in so many ways than Ashley, and I am so proud of her and her work. She is an artist who expresses herself through so many forms, all of which she does with amazing success. Ashley takes great pride in every project she undertakes, making sure it reflects well on her and those it represents. And for this project, she has, once again, captured exactly what I wished to convey: There is only so much sand in the hourglass, and time with aging parents is quickly running out. Ashley cheers me on in so many ways, and I am so thankful to have her in my life.

Ladies, my hat is off to both of you. I can never repay you for the ways you have brought this book into its final formation. Many thanks for the ways you have, respectively, understood my mission and intent and have combined your talents to culminate this project in an appealing and masterful form.

CONTENTS

INTRODUCTION 1
CHAPTER ONE 5
    Honor or Obedience? 6
    Displaying Honor Through Love and Care 9
    Sanctity of Life and Displaying Honor Through Support 12
    Honoring Parents in the Face of Opposition 15
    Remember, Not All Battles Are Worth Fighting 16
    Do Not Patronize or Infantilize Your Aging Parent . 19
    When Should I Oppose My Parent? What If My Aging Parent Opposes Me? 22

CHAPTER TWO 29
    Can I Honor My Parents and Disobey Them? 30
    Can I Obey My Parents and Still Dishonor Them? Can I Honor My Parents and Still Dishonor Them? . 35

CHAPTER THREE 42
    Be Cautious of Creating Unnecessary Dependence . 44
    Watch for Over-Commitment 45
    Where Needs End and Wants Begin 48
    Questions to Consider 49

CHAPTER FOUR 54
   Distinguishing Needs from Wants 56
   Identifying and Dealing with Manipulative
   Behaviors 57
   Blaming, Accusing, Whining, and Complaining 60
   Other Difficult Behaviors 67
   Tools for Disarming Difficult Behaviors 69
CHAPTER FIVE 78
   Showing Sensitivity to Loss 79
   Coping with Loss 83
CONCLUSION 90
BIBLICAL REFERENCES 93
REFERENCES 100
   Additional Resources 101

No, Mom!

Can I Tell My Aging Parents "No" and Still Honor Them?

INTRODUCTION

I remember the day I looked in the mirror and saw my mother staring back at me…YIKES! It had come true: I had turned into my mother! I've heard it said that no matter how hard you fight it, daughters are destined to turn into their mothers. Likewise, sons are bound to become like their fathers. If what happened to me is any indication, this prediction is accurate. My oldest daughter has now reached an age where she has embraced her lot and has accepted her destiny. We laugh about our similar attitudes, phrases, and mannerisms. Bless her heart, her future lies before her. My younger daughter, on the other hand, has not yet come to the realization, that fight as she will, the struggle is futile. Some lessons in life must be learned the hard way.

Although we laugh—or not—about turning into our parents, the influence parents have on their children is profound and biblically ordained. As God designed, parents are commanded to have a venerating influence upon their children. For example, Ephesians 6:4 says, "And you, fathers, do not provoke your children to wrath, but bring them up in the training and admonition of the Lord." Also Proverbs 29:17 tells Christians, "Correct your son, and he will give you rest; yes, he will give delight to your soul," and Colossians 3:21 says, "Fathers, do not provoke your children, lest they become discouraged." Likewise, children have biblical responsibilities to honor, respect, and care for their parents throughout their lives.

In my forty-plus years of ministry, I have never met an adult child who intentionally desired to mistreat, disrespect, or dishonor their aging parents. Quite the contrary. Most adult children desire a loving and harmonious relationship with their parents, even those whose relationships have historically been fraught with conflict, misunderstanding, or worse, a feeling of ambivalence. In other words, whether past experiences with our parents are positive or negative, the connection with our parents has been ordained by God. Thus, we are commanded to honor and cherish our parents despite the hurts and frustrations we may have experienced in the past or are currently experiencing.

What I have found is that, although adult children desire to care for and about their aging parents in an honorable and respectful way, they are often faced with never-before-encountered situations that challenge their knowledge and ability to do so. They have never been faced with the physical and mental frailties that often accompany aging and are not prepared for the growing care needs their aging parents will be requiring.

Sometimes, throughout the aging parent-adult child relationship, situations may arise that give the adult child reason to pause and ask the question: "Can I tell Mom (or Dad) "no" and still be respectful and honoring to them?" I remember, years ago as a young, married adult, one

Sunday the lesson in Sunday School being on honoring our parents. Even though I was not the teacher, I posed this question to the group: "Can we honor our parents and still disobey them…can we tell our parents "No?" One male classmate, Mike—who was nearing 30 years old—started to squirm in his seat and finally said, "I don't even want to go there." His mother, like mine, was the disciplinarian in the family—and she even scared me—so I could understand Mike's trepidation at the mere thought of going against his mother.

But the question remains: "Can adult children tell their aging parents 'no' and still honor them?"

All relationships can be complex, and yet none so much as the aging parent-adult child relationship. As in all aspects of life, the Bible gives direction and instruction on how to appropriately love and care for aging parents. We are commanded to honor and, in some instances, obey our parents. These instructions will be explored in their correct contexts to assist in the common struggle of emotionally and spiritually caring for aging parents.

The names of all references to individuals have been changed to protect their privacy.

Unless otherwise noted, all scripture references are from the New King James Version. A complete list of Scriptures used in this book can be found under the Biblical References section at the end.

CHAPTER ONE

What is the Difference between Honoring My Aging Parents and Obeying Them?

As children growing up in church, we are taught the Ten Commandments, the fifth of which states "Children, honor your father and mother that your days may be long upon the land which the LORD your God is giving you" (Exodus 20:12). Not only are we taught that truth in church, but it is likely that our parents may have conveniently reminded us of that commandment when we were disobedient as children because obedience is usually a manifestation of honor.

Thank goodness my mother took me to Sunday School where I was taught this biblical truth, along with numerous other stories of the Bible. As a child, I enjoyed Sunday School. It was an important aspect of my spiritual development, much more than the worship service where I had to sit still and be quiet. That is not to say I didn't learn certain biblical "truths" because of my attendance at the worship service. Often I was escorted out of the worship service, which our family called "Big Church," on many occasions for misbehavior. This "carrying out" process usually resulted in various degrees of discipline designed to make sure the commandment to "honor (obey) your mother" was reinforced. (Trust me, several of those punishments were lessons I have not forgotten!)

For minor children, the words "honoring" and "obeying" are easily connected. As adult children, however, it is important to understand the difference between honor and obedience. While often taught (and thought) to be interchangeable, the nuance of the words can cause confusion and leave room for misinterpretation, often making communication between adult children and their aging parents unnecessarily complicated. The importance and validation of biblical commands of when and how to honor and obey parents goes beyond a scriptural definition of the words. So, the questions are, "What is the difference between honor and obedience?" "Can I, as an adult child, honor my parents without obeying them?" "If so, under what circumstances?" And "What happens if my parents oppose me?" (YIKES!)

Honor or Obedience?

My mother's teaching, reinforced by my Sunday School teachers, that obedience is a manifestation of honor was not wrong. Small children must be taught to obey their parents and children must learn to comply and be obedient to the instructions of their parents. Even though children of all ages will test their parents' resolve and authority, even in their simple ways, they can learn to understand what it means to love in the Lord and to obey His commands as demonstrated by honoring and obeying their parents. As a result, children tend to grow up believing the words "honor" and "obey" can, and should, be used interchangeably. This can become problematic in adulthood as the two words do not mean the same thing and are not interchangeable.

The biblical difference between the words "honor" and "obey" needs to be clarified so that adult children can appropriately understand not only their responsibility for their aging parent but how God intends for that responsibility to be carried out. It is surprisingly easy for the two words to become convoluted and misconstrued, making it difficult for adult children to separate "honor" and "obey" due to their early teaching in the church. Without this understanding, as children mature into adulthood, rarely is the distinction made between the two words, leaving adult children believing that if they are going to honor their parents, they must obey them. This interchangeable use of the two words can further complicate an already complex situation.

For the sake of definition, obeying is doing (or not doing) what you are told to do, going (or not going) where you are told to go; honoring is demonstrating respect and admiration, caring by showing affection, and prizing someone highly. Perhaps the easiest way to understand the difference between "honor" and "obey" is this: Obeying is doing what you are told to do; honoring is the attitude with which you do it. For example, you may mow Mom's yard or pick up her groceries every week as she requests but do it begrudgingly or with complaint. This is much the same concept as Paul talks about in 2 Corinthians 9:6-7 when he writes, "But this I say: He who sows sparingly will also reap sparingly, and he who sows bountifully will also reap bountifully. So let each one give as he purposes in his heart, not grudgingly or of necessity; for God loves a cheerful giver." Paul instructs Christians to give (or do) as they have decided in their heart, not reluctantly or under compulsion (begrudgingly), but with a cheerful heart, which pleases the Lord.

Whereas children are commanded to *honor* parents in Exodus, in Ephesians 6:1 the Apostle Paul calls children to *obey* their parents when he writes, "Children, obey your parents in the Lord, for this is right." Minor children are called to obey their parents as a demonstration of respect and familial order, provided the parental instructions do not require the child to sin. On the other hand, adult children are commanded to honor their parents—which also includes respect—but does not necessarily dictate that they obey their parents, particularly if the parent asks the adult child to do something that is harmful or sinful.

In contrast to Paul's writing to the Ephesians, which was intended for the instruction for minor children, Dr. Charlie Trimm, Assistant Professor of Biblical and Theological Studies at Biola University, interprets the command for children to honor their parents in Exodus 20:12 and Deuteronomy 5:16 as one directed primarily to adult children, requiring them to care for elderly parents as an indication of honor and respect. This supports the notion that the terms honoring and obeying are not intended to be interchangeable once children reach adulthood.

Displaying Honor Through Love and Care

Honoring parents involves cherishing them, caring for and about them, and showing them respect. Accepting personal idiosyncrasies, as hard as that may be, and giving affirmation not only shows honor and respect but also prevents resentment from infiltrating the relationship. Although adult children may or may not share the beliefs and values of their parents, it is important that the beliefs and values of aging parents be affirmed and respected in deference to those of the adult child.

For example, if aging parents feel strongly that Sunday should be a day of rest, it would be best if adult children helping to mow the lawn could arrange to undertake that task another day, if possible. Even the everyday use of language (which has changed dramatically in the past few years) can be disrespectful and dishonoring to aging parents. In my childhood, offensive language was not tolerated by my parents. My husband and I, likewise, raised our children not to use those words. Now that they are grown and outside of our influence (and earshot), it is not known what language is used in the privacy of their homes. However, out of respect and honor for their father and me, even as adults, obscenities are not freely spoken in our home by our children.

Developing an understanding of, and respecting, the parental belief system, and even idiosyncrasies, is not only a form of honoring parents, it also serves to validate the lives of aging parents. In addition, it is important that aging parents experience a sense of recognition of purpose and meaning in having lived. Like housework, parenting is often a thankless job. It is expected that tasks will be done, homework completed, values instilled, work ethics ingrained, and sound advice given. Just as people like to be acknowledged for a job well done at work or appreciated for assistance offered, it is nice when adult children can look back, see the constructive ways parents have impacted their lives and tell them how their influence has positively shaped their lives.

Not only are validating and respecting the parental belief systems (and how those have impacted the lives of the adult children emotionally) beneficial to the aging parent, there is also value in understanding how those belief systems came into being. Therefore, and perhaps more importantly for the adult child, sitting down with parents and asking questions about facts—and feelings—surrounding life events can draw a picture that helps explain behaviors, beliefs, and values, especially those that may seem peculiar. Most likely, there is a reason why Mom and Dad behave the way they do, hold the beliefs they do, and fervently hang on to certain possessions. Understanding life experiences can be valuable in explaining the reasons behind behaviors and beliefs.

Failure to have these conversations results in lost opportunities to connect to aging parents on a deeper, intimate level. Conversations that engage the parent in life review also provide children with a window into their family history and culture. Although perhaps seemingly unimportant at a time when the stressors of caregiving demands are overwhelming, the loss of family history that aging parents could have provided cannot be retrieved once the parents die or the ravages of dementia set in.

In addition to time constraints associated with caregiving and everyday life, there may be several other reasons children do not engage aging parents in life review conversations. Perhaps there is fear of causing emotional distress by uncovering or discussing unpleasant situations that the child feels incapable of, or unwilling to, deal with. For example, maybe there is a history of abuse, financial ruin, incest, incarceration, or countless other scandalous circumstances that may have brought shame upon the family.

Unresolved issues between the adult child and the parent may also be barriers to having honest and comfortable conversations. Geographical distance may also seem to be an obstacle to establishing or maintaining close relationships. Although these intimate conversations are probably best and most comfortably conducted face-to-face, the use of technology can allow aging parents and adult children to connect.

In some cases, there may even be family secrets that make asking appropriate life review questions impossible because the children do not even know to ask about certain subjects. As an example, several years ago, an elderly woman came to me needing to make a confession: She had had a baby out of wedlock and a family member had raised the child as their own. She was preparing to inform her other children and she was asking for my blessing and support. Her other children were in for quite the surprise, yet, hopefully, they could understand and appreciate the position their mother found herself in once Mom provided an explanation. Not only is this a good example of a family secret, but it also indicates the need for resolution that occurs in old age.

It would be nice—maybe idyllic would be a better word—to assume that the aging parent/adult child relationship is primarily a positive one. Past hurts and misunderstandings that have not been forgiven or resolved often stand in the way of constructive conversations and important life review encounters. Despite Dad's gruff exterior, or Mom's hurtful criticisms, just like the elderly woman who needed to confess her past, parents have a strong need to resolve issues before they die. Consider this a teaser for another book, as issues of resolution and end-of-life care are too vast and complicated to adequately address in this book. Suffice it to say, however, that there can be topics of life review, such as school year recollections, favorite memories of childhood, or attributes they appreciated about their own parents, that are innocuous yet could lead aging parents and their adult children in the direction of resolution.

Sanctity of Life and Displaying Honor Through Support

Beyond the terms "honor" and "obey," adult Christian children are compelled to consider the sanctity of life of their aging parents. Because Man is created in the image of God making him capable of having a relationship with God, He commands and expects life be valued at all ages. In addition, the Psalmist acknowledges that we are known even in our mother's womb, that we are fearfully and wonderfully made, and that the days were fashioned for us when as yet there were none of them.

The God who created His children in the womb also cares for, protects, and rescues them throughout life, even until old age. Isaiah wrote, "God says, 'Even to your old age, I am He, and even to gray hairs I will carry you!" (Isaiah 46:4) There is no time in life that God does not value and care for His people.

Scripture further reveals the value Jesus placed on man, making man's importance above the birds (Matthew 6:26) and worldly goods (Matthew 16:26). The value placed on mankind is not contingent upon behavior, performance, or works. In fact, Jesus died for the sins of mankind despite his failings, and there is no greater love (John 15:13). The Scripture does not refer to any devaluing of man due to age or infirmity.

Fulfilling the command to honor the sanctity of life goes hand-in-glove with the command to honor parents, making the case that the command for honor involves the support of parents. To look at it another way, this type of honor requires that children not desert, forsake, or abandon their parents.

Desertion or abandonment can take several forms. The most obvious transgression of this form of dishonor is the failure to keep in contact with aging parents.

Closely linked with that is ensuring the well-being of parents, including their physical needs (nutritional, housing, medical, and safety), emotional needs (giving and receiving affection, acceptance, validation, and security), social needs (friendship, a sense of belonging, empathy, and trust), and spiritual needs (faith, prayer, giving, and acts of love and mercy) are met. Often, these needs can be met by helping them with grocery shopping or picking up medications from the pharmacy, providing transportation to the doctor, changing light bulbs, doing yard work or household chores, and ensuring they get to religious services as desired. It also requires establishing or maintaining a sense of trust, as well as the expressions of love and acceptance. Additionally, aging parents often may need financial assistance with monthly bills or housing expenses.

These are easy words to say, but putting them into practice can get quite overwhelming, expensive, and even complicated. What if Mom can't afford her medication? Are her children on the hook to pay? According to God's examples that require honoring the sanctity of life, the answer is yes. What if Mom needs a place to live? Are the children required to provide—or at a minimum assist with—housing costs or arrangements? According to God's command to honor—and not desert—parents, the answer is yes.

Here's an even more complicated situation: What if Mom needs financial assistance, or worse, a place to live because she has a gambling or shopping addiction and does not manage her funds (which otherwise would be adequate) well? Are adult children required to provide support in the case of sinful behavior? (YIKES!)

According to Dr. Don Owsley, Pastoral Counselor, the command to honor parents is still required of adult children even in the case of repeated bad judgment or sinful behavior. However, the way the honor is bestowed may change considering willful, sinful behavior. He explained it to me like this: "Children must still honor their aging parent but must find other avenues in which that honor is expressed." In other words, under normal circumstances of true need, adult children have an obligation to support their parents. However, it is not the adult child's responsibility to rescue parents from the consequences of their poor life choices nor to enable them to continue in their sin, such as by enabling their parents by paying their rent or mortgage—or even by taking the parents into their home where the parents have no financial responsibility for household expenses. Nevertheless, children can, and must, still express honor by respecting the parent in other ways, such as being honest and respectful in communications, demonstrating appreciation for love and care, and providing care and assistance circumspect of potential sin. This explanation limits and directs the adult child's responsibility to one of honor yet does not require participation or rescue from the aging parent's sinful behavior.

Honoring Parents in the Face of Opposition

Being in opposition to parents is an uncomfortable position to be in. Again, childhood lessons of honor and obedience come to mind in instances when your parents not only disagree with you but may even stand against you. Do you stand down and acquiesce to their wishes, ideas, or desires? Do you stand firm in your position, despite the hurt or rift that may develop to prove a point? Do you correct your parent, to do what you believe to be best, perhaps even attempting to bring them back to reality in the case of dementia?

How do we find a common ground, both honoring our parents and their values, without dishonoring ourselves? This can be a sticky-wicket and requires the laying of some groundwork before fully addressing the question, "What if my parents oppose me?"

To answer that question, the following topics need to be addressed:

1. How to choose which battles are worth engaging aging parents in
2. How to avoid patronizing aging parents, regardless of dementia or seemingly poor judgement
3. How to respectfully manage opposition by aging parents

Remember, Not All Battles Are Worth Fighting

Have you ever been in a conversation with someone who always had to be right? It didn't matter what the topic was, they had the right answer, knew what was best, had the only solution on how to do things correctly, and insisted everyone see things their way? I don't know about you, but it doesn't take me long to get my fill of those conversations.

I look at social media—rarely do I participate in it—and I see people I love (and who love each other) in open, public conflict over ridiculous disagreements involving topics such as societal changes and political positions. As a result of their conflict, they often "unfriend" each other and will even cut off contact outside of social media. How those ugly remarks, meaningless conflicts, and resulting estrangements make me long for the simple days of childhood when our biggest disagreements were over who was going to be "it" in a game of tag.

In the grand scheme of things, if you think about most conflicts, is being "right" or being on the "winning side" paramount? Must everything go our way? Even if we believe we are right, can we allow someone to be wrong without going to battle over it? The truth of the matter is, when it comes to relationships, especially relationships with the people we love, our goal should be to "win the war." What is the "war?" In this case, simply put, the war is maintaining a sense of honor and respect, of love and compassion, with those we love. To do this, we must remember we do not need to win every battle. Many wars have been won despite battles being lost.

Another way of looking at this is to ask the question: Is it possible to disagree with my aging parent without engaging them in an argument? I hope the answer is yes.

There is nothing wrong with differing opinions and minor disagreements. However, despite our convoluted belief that an argument is like a debate where there is a winner and a loser, that is not true. When an argument ensues, even if there appears to be an apparent winner, relationships suffer, and everyone loses.

So, adult children need to tamp down that competitive nature that desires to be right and to win, and instead realize which situations are merely trivial irritations that have no overall significance to the physical, spiritual, or emotional well-being of their aging parent. It costs nothing to concede an argument (hopefully, before it even gets revved up) and the payoff is well worth the minor bruise the adult child may feel to their ego.

I remember the day Margaret, the daughter of a resident in the long-term care facility where I worked, came to talk to me about her elderly mother who was experiencing dementia. She told me about an argument she had had with her mom over where the mother was living. It seems her mother believed she was in Ironton, Ohio (where, in fact, she had lived at one point). Margaret insisted her mother understand she was living in Ironton, Missouri, and thus the argument ensued. Was this really a battle worth engaging in? I asked Margaret, "How important is it that your mother realize she is in Ironton, Missouri rather than Ironton, Ohio?" Margaret paused to think for a moment. I said, "The days are short, Margaret. This is not the time to be in conflict with your mother. Instead, this is the time to love and enjoy your mother." I suggested to Margaret that rather than correcting her mother about where she was living, she might say something such as, "We really had some good times when we lived in Ironton, Ohio, didn't we, Mom? What is your favorite memory of living there?"

Hopefully, this example indicates how unnecessary it is to engage an aging parent in a silly argument. (This almost bordered on picking a fight, it was so insignificant.) Rather than jeopardizing a relationship by turning a disagreement into an argument, the daughter could so easily have used the conversation as an opportunity for life review and validation of a life well lived. If nothing else is gleaned from this chapter, remember that arguing is not the proper tactic for winning the war.

Do Not Patronize or Infantilize Your Aging Parent

Rarely have I met a person (of any age) who wants to be told what to do. In anticipation of beginning kindergarten, my five-year old granddaughter did not seem particularly excited about her upcoming new adventure. When I asked her why she wasn't eager to go to kindergarten, she replied, "I don't want to be bossed." Even at an early age, autonomy is an important manifestation of self-determination. If a five-year old doesn't want to be bossed, imagine how much more so aging parents resent being "bossed!" Nobody wants to be told what to do, especially by someone whose diapers they changed. Thus, parents may become resistive—sometimes even combative—when they believe their autonomy and sense of independence and control is being threatened.

I have often heard adult children say the roles have reversed with their aging parents. "I am now the parent, and they are the child." That is far from the truth! Even though parents may become physically dependent—and may even exhibit child-like behavior—the parent does not become the child. When we are children, we do not have the life experiences of an adult. Even aging parents with dementia retain adult life experiences. To treat an aging parent as a child by talking down to them or using a tone as if they were a child, is dishonoring and patronizing. Excluding them from conversations or opportunities for decision-making strips aging parents of their sense of autonomy and purpose.

In other words, adult children should not come in guns a'blazing and expect to take over. At all stages of life, people need to experience a sense of control over what happens to them. Do not assume that, just because they are old, aging parents do not have opinions, cannot participate in decisions, or want to be rescued. Talk to them and address them with respect due adults.

Calling an older adult using a pet name not historically used with them, such as "sweetheart," can also be patronizing. Adult children should call their parents by the name they have always used (Mom, Mother, Dad, Father); other caregivers should respectfully use their preferred name (or their appropriate title, such as Mr., Mrs., Miss, Doctor, Reverend, etc.). If well-meaning caregivers are overheard calling an aging parent by a pet name, it is appropriate for adult children to intervene and gently ask that the caregiver use their parent's proper name. Not only are children called to honor their parents, they must also ensure that others treat their parents with honor and respect.

For many aging parents, they have enjoyed—and expect to continue enjoying—an appreciation for their good judgment and sound advice. Even in her advanced stage of dementia, I would still consult with my mother over problems I was experiencing. Those problems ranged from family issues to frustrations I was experiencing in my feeble attempts to sew. Sometimes she gave simple but sound advice. Sometimes it just took telling her about my problems for me to imagine how she would have dealt with them. Once I "talked it over" with her, I would convey my thoughts with her, and she would smile.

My mother lived in the long-term care facility where I was administrator. Despite being unable to remember many things due to her dementia, it seemed she always knew how to find my office. Unless I was in a meeting with clients or guests, the staff knew to just let her come in. One day she arrived while I was conducting a staff meeting. As she came in, the staff moved over to give her a seat, and the meeting continued. Periodically, I would say, "What do you think about that idea, Mom?" or "Do you think we should do that, Mom?" Mind you, she really had little conception of what was being discussed. She would usually just agree, responding, "I think that's a good idea," and we would move on. At the conclusion of the meeting, after everyone had left, she said to me, "That was fun. I want to do this again." I'd say, "You bet, Mom. You had some great ideas, and I appreciated your input."

If someone with advanced dementia can appreciate being consulted and included in problem-solving, imagine how much more an aging parent of sound mind would experience a sense of purpose and meaning in being included and involved in the lives of their children. Do not assume that age—even accompanied by dementia—diminishes the need to be included or involved. Ask for their opinion; ask for their advice; and then thank them for it, even if you disagree or don't follow it.

When Should I Oppose My Parent? What If My Aging Parent Opposes Me?

Here we are at a big question: How do I handle opposition with my aging parent? Standing in opposition to parents should only occur in necessary situations where adult children are striving to honorably care for, and about, their aging parents. Situations involving disagreements over the safety and well-being of aging parents are certainly examples of potential conflict where parents may oppose decisions being offered or made on their behalf. Other, more trivial situations are not worthy of the needless strife the disagreements will cause. In other words, there may be a proper time that necessitates opposition, but it is not *every* time.

Perhaps the parent is no longer safe living alone or the maintenance of the house has become overwhelming and unmanageable, however, the parent refuses to move or allow a caregiver or homemaker to come in to assist them. Maybe driving has become a serious safety concern as evidenced by repeated fender benders, yet the parent insists on continuing to drive. Perhaps bills are going unpaid and collection notices are arriving in the mail, but the parent will not allow anyone to assist them with managing their finances. These are examples of major concerns adult children experience. They are also common responses of aging parents that present roadblocks and challenges for adult children trying to honor and support their parents.

Change, even small change, is never easy. And it seems like the older we get, the harder it is to adapt. So, unless the parent is in imminent danger, there is time for most situations—even those that may seem trivial—to be talked over. It is always better when the parent can make the choice rather than a decision being made for them or forced on them. For example, something as innocuous as moving a small object in the parent's home to another spot because it would be safer should not be done without discussing it with them. After all, it is possible the object is placed in that particular place for a reason.

Expressing love and concern, along with discussing emotions and possible options for dealing with unsafe or undesirable situations reaffirms the adult child's commitment to honor the parent, provides an opportunity to engage the parent in problem-solving, and gives the parent a sense of control over their life. Immediately "putting the hammer down" on parents without allowing for discussion, or even time to adjust to a new idea or situation, is bound to create opposition.

When adult children empathetically consider the position of the parent, they can better understand how changes associated with opposition represent a loss and a sense of being out of control. It may take a little time to adjust to the idea of moving or allowing someone else—potentially a stranger—in the house to help with chores. It is not easy to give up independence and freedom by handing over the car keys. Finances are a private matter, especially for aging parents who were taught that you did not discuss financial matters with anyone but your spouse. Permitting someone to take over the handling of financial matters may feel like a violation of their privacy. In fact, the two greatest symbols of independence are the car keys and the checkbook or credit card. When those are taken away, for many older adults, their autonomy and the sense of control over their life has also been taken away.

Being sensitive to the effects of change will facilitate, and alleviate, a degree of potential opposition. That is not to say that aging parents won't dig in their heels and flat out refuse to allow change or consider the concerns adult children express. However, if a trusting relationship that is empathic to the emotions associated with loss is in place, the parent is more likely to be receptive and allow necessary changes to be made.

I remember the day Anna became a new resident at the long-term care facility where I was the administrator. She was nearly blind, and she was frightened. And she was out the door, lickity-split! The staff came to tell me that Anna was outside, and they couldn't get her back in. To make matters worse, they had contacted the doctor, who advised them to call the police to forcibly load her up and take her to the hospital for a psychiatric evaluation. This was an already bad situation now headed for disaster! The number one thing we needed to accomplish was for Anna to trust us. That was not going to happen if we took the advice of the doctor.

I told another staff person to bring a wheelchair and follow me outside. I wanted the wheelchair to be in the wings, and I had all the staff back away while I went to talk to Anna. When I found her, she was on her hands and knees weeding the border around the building. I got down on my hands and knees and started helping her. At first, I didn't say anything, I just weeded alongside of her. Then I started talking about how she had, I imagine, always been a hard worker. She, in turn, told me how proud her parents had been of her work ethic.

I moved the conversation to acknowledging her fear and not knowing who to trust. Then I expressed the concern of the staff that she was outside. I eventually—and honestly—shared with her the suggestion that had been made for the police to take her to the hospital. In her European accent, she said, "I will punch them in the nose!" I replied, "You could do that. But I don't think it will achieve the result you desire." We continued to pull weeds. I finally said, "I don't want you to have to go to the hospital. What do you think about coming inside with me?" She said, "I will work to the end of the row, and then we will go inside." When we got to the end of the row, I motioned for the wheelchair to be brought closer. She got into the wheelchair and peacefully went into the building. From that day forward, Anna trusted me and would allow me to be involved in her care in ways she would not allow others. Just imagine how things would have been different if her opposition to the staff had been met with a police ride to the hospital.

Although Anna was not my parent, the example of dealing with opposition from an aging individual is fitting. I did not go outside and tell her she had to come in. I did not rush her. I met her where she was, emotionally and physically. Once I had garnered her trust, she cooperated with me, not just that day, but in the days following.

Just as I had been honest with Anna and had acknowledged her fears and emotions, adult children should take the same approach with changes facing their aging parents. For example, acknowledging the values and beliefs surrounding financial information and the violation of privacy Dad feels at his children nosing into his finances will go a long way to achieving his cooperation. It is dishonoring for a child to come in and yank away the checkbook, which represents yanking away independence, autonomy, and control. Ask for Dad's cooperation rather than demand it. Metaphorically speaking, it is unnecessary for the "police" to be called to haul Dad away as a first resort, rather than a last.

It is possible that Mom does not necessarily wish to be contrary. Perhaps she refuses to move out of her house because she fears the house will be sold (and it might). It is possible that the house represents memories of a time when she felt needed by her children, when she had a purpose. Maybe the house is a status symbol of the hard work she and her husband endured to achieve it. Maybe she desires to leave the house to her children as an inheritance and fears that sentiment is in jeopardy. Perhaps the idea of changing to something unfamiliar, or the notion of moving a lifetime of accumulated belonging and treasures, is simply overwhelming. Acknowledging these emotions will help the adult child understand the motivation behind the opposition.

To fully achieve this understanding, children not only need to listen to the words their parents are saying, but they must also hear the meanings and emotions behind the words. This type of listening requires empathy. How would I respond if I felt threatened, distrustful, or angry? I might respond the same way. In addition, most children know their parents. They know their history, and they have spent a lifetime watching how their parents have coped with adversity. They know what pushes their buttons, both positively and negatively. Adult children can use this knowledge to assist in garnering cooperation and finding potential alternatives to difficult situations.

A number of years ago, my mother was especially angry with me. She was in the early to moderate stages of

Alzheimer's disease but maintained an awareness of my attention (or in this case, lack of attention) to her. Even though I visited her daily, she accused me of having time for everyone but her. Rather than refuting the accusation (and engaging her in an argument), I acknowledged her feeling of being neglected by me. Then, I helped her recall times in her working career when her boss called upon her to perform an important task.

"Mom, you were the one he called on because he knew you could do [this task] better than anyone else. So, when he called on you, you dropped everything else to help him, didn't you?" "That's right, I did!" she responded. "Well, what if that is how my job works, too? There are certain tasks I must perform, and sometimes those tasks keep me away from you, which I regret." "Well, I can understand that," she said. By helping Mom recall situations from her past, she was able to relate to events happening in my life that had a negative effect on her, and she could forgive my (seeming) neglect of her.

Children need a quiver full of arrows to use when confronting issues of controversy. These arrows include being honest and patient, honoring and respecting values and beliefs, validating emotions, and discovering and understanding what motivates parental behaviors.

CHAPTER TWO
Can I Honor My Parents and Disobey Them? Can I Obey My Parents and Still Dishonor Them?

Now that the difference between "honoring" and "obeying" has been established, it is important to understand the manner adult children are called to interact with their parents needs, requests, and (sometimes) demands. In other words, how can we—and when should we—tell our parents "no" if their requests are ill-advised, unreasonable, or unsafe? And how can this be done in ways still that convey honor and preserve dignity?

I remember the first time I ever told my mother, "No." Of course, I had previously opposed her (as is common in adolescence) and had even had the occasional disagreement over the mothering of my children. However, those instances were different than the day I flat out said, "No, Mom, I'm not going to do that."

My mother was well-known for her scathing letters. My brothers were frequent recipients of these letters, as were legislators and governors of various states. When the scathing letter failed to achieve the desired result, she often sought out someone—usually me—to champion her cause. She called me one day to tell me about a disagreement she was experiencing with one of my brothers, and said, "I want you to call him and tell him he should respect my position in the family as the matriarch and drive me to visit my sister even if his wife objects." I quickly thought through the ramifications of my involvement in this conflict and concluded it was not in my best interest to jump in the middle. So, I gently said, "No, Mom, I'm not going to do that because I do not believe it is wise." Although I did not give her an explanation of *why* I was not going to do that, I did make another offer, saying, "However, I will tell him of your concern about your sister and suggest he talk with you about it," to assist with the conflict resolution. Because of my alternative offer — which she found very acceptable — my mother accepted my refusal of her request, not as a rejection but as support. WHEW!

Can I Honor My Parents and Disobey Them?

Maybe a better question is: Can I honor my parents, disobey them, and still please God? While the concept of achieving honor through disobedience sounds antithetical, there is a beautiful example of this very thing in the Old Testament book of Ruth. The story contained in Ruth 1:6-17 demonstrates the difference between honor and obedience and is an example of how adult children can honor parents by obeying as well as honor them by disobeying.

Following the death of her two sons, Naomi, an Israelite, entreated her two daughters-in-law, who were Moabites, to return to their mothers' homes. In obedience, one daughter-in-law, Orpah, honoring the wishes of her mother-in-law, kissed Naomi and left for home. In contrast, Naomi's other daughter-in-law, Ruth, clung to Naomi and pledged herself to stay with her mother-in-law and to care for her despite being released from the marital and moral responsibility of care. In this way, Ruth honored Naomi through what could be considered disobedience to her mother-in-law's instructions. This illustration from the Bible clearly identifies obedience and honor as separate commands and likewise provides support and justification for the occasion when adult children may be unable to obey the wishes and desires of parents.

In his book *Caregiving from Your Spiritual Strengths*, Dr. Richard Johnson addresses what honor looks like in the caregiving setting, again acknowledging that "honor" does not mean "obey" as adult children and caregivers cannot obey all requests in a "simplistic obedience," particularly when the request is something that cannot be obliged. Instead, Johnson promotes honor as a recognition of respect that results from coming to genuinely know and appreciate the aging parent as a manifestation of God's love and care. Thus, parental honor can be achieved even when the adult child disobeys the wishes of the parent, a notion that is often a stumbling block for adult children because it goes against childhood teachings.

There are times when adult children and caregivers cannot obey every request in a simplistic obedience, particularly when the request is something that cannot, or should not, be obliged. For example, what if Mom asks you to make a promise you may not be able to keep? Many adult children have been told, "Promise me you will never put me away in a nursing home," or "Promise me you will never let me suffer, that you will help me hasten my death." These are tough—and real—situations adult children may face in caring for aging parents.

As a matter of safety, what if Dad insists on continuing to drive, even when it is obviously unsafe for him to do so? Can the keys be "taken away" in an honoring way? I remember when my mother was no longer capable of driving due to dementia. Despite her increasing forgetfulness, she still remembered the pleasure of driving. She would say, "I don't understand why they won't let me drive." Because of her dementia, I did not attempt to reason with her about her inability to drive, but rather I made statements and asked questions of interest such as, "If you had the car keys and could take off driving, where would you go?" and "When you were able to drive, you felt FREE! Now, you feel trapped?" Usually, this topic would conclude by my expressions of sadness at her loss. She would accept that, and we moved on...until the next time. Then, we had the same conversation all over again. The point is, there was no sense in arguing about whether Mom could drive.

If driving is unsafe, for example, have a conversation that expresses love and concern in a respectful manner. In the event of driving and physical limitations, the conversation may focus on concerns regarding safety, sadness at the loss of independence, alternative means of transportation to medical appointments and church, and ways to access necessary supplies. By acknowledging subjective concerns and emotions (safety, grief, loss, etc.), objective needs and obstacles (transportation, groceries and medications, etc.) can be respectfully addressed. These types of conversations preserve dignity surrounding the loss of independence and control.

Some aging parents recognize losses that have occurred, or impending losses that are looming in the near future. They will bless their adult children by saying things such as, "I am no longer safe driving," or "I do not think I should continue living alone." Sometimes the transition happens naturally when children start driving parents to appointments or picking them up for church. Maybe home maintenance has become overwhelming or unsafe and the children have assumed the majority of the maintenance responsibilities. When these honest conversations happen, it demonstrates the wisdom of the aging parent, and it takes the burden off the adult child who is often put in the position of being the bad guy who takes away the car keys or talks of moving Mom from her home.

But, what if this transition does not go so smoothly? What if Dad refuses to hand over the keys? Maybe he becomes belligerent, and the scene turns ugly. "I've driven for 70 years and have *never* had an accident!" "I taught YOU to drive! There's no way I'm going to let you tell me I can't drive!" Maybe Mom retorts, "Who do you think you are, coming into my house and dictating what I can and can't do?" Or worse, what if Dad or Mom accuses saying, "You were taught to honor your parents…you call this HONOR?? I've never been so dishonored in my life!"

Here is the *real* test of honor. Although it may feel like a hurtful, personal attack, it is not wise to engage in a like response. Retaliating in anger will only fan the flames. Difficult as it may be, the better approach would be to calmly acknowledge the hurt, anger, fear that Dad is experiencing. Providing validation for a good driving record and appreciation for the driving lessons is also a good approach. "It hurts you to think I am taking away your independence." "You have driven for many years, and you taught me well. Thank you." After that discussion, it is time to express love and concern for safety, perhaps giving examples of unsafe situations. "I do not wish to strip you of your independence, and I know driving provides you with freedom to come and go as you please. However, I was alarmed when [this happened]. And then [this happened]. I hope you can understand my concern because I love you very much."

If Dad continues to resist, it might be advisable to enlist the help of an unbiased authority figure, such as his doctor. Attend the next doctor's appointment and inform the doctor of what has transpired with regards to Dad's ability to drive. Do not hide from Dad what you plan to do or lie to him, and do not shame him for his resistance. Simply ask the doctor what he or she would advise.

Although the inability to drive and the removal of the car keys was used as an example of situations where adult children must intervene for the sake of safety, there are countless other scenarios that require adult children to disobey to honor their parents. Just as an example, if Dad insists on cleaning out the gutters but is tottery and a fall risk, perhaps the ladder needs to be removed from the property—along with the promise that someone will clean the gutters at whatever interval Dad had previously been doing it. However, as will be discussed in the next section, doing the right thing with the wrong approach or attitude can still result in dishonor.

Can I Obey My Parents and Still Dishonor Them? Can I Honor My Parents and Still Dishonor Them?

Yes, adult children can obey their parents and still dishonor them. A well-known biblical example of dishonor in the face of obedience is the parable of the prodigal son found in Luke 15:11-32. While the younger son requests, receives, and squanders away his inheritance, the elder, dutiful son remains at home, fulfilling his familial duties to his father. Yet, when the younger son returns home broken and repentant, the elder son is angry with his father for restoring his brother's position in the family. Although there are many sermons to be preached about this story, for the purposes of understanding obedience and dishonor, it serves well as an example.

There are two common ways adult children can obey their parents and still dishonor them. The first way involves adult children ignoring obvious signs that parents need help and subsequently failing to interject themselves into situations that may be uncomfortable but that require attention or advice. The second way adult children can obey parents and still dishonor them is with the attitudes with which they communicate, provide care, or perform tasks intended to benefit their aging parents.

With regards to ignoring signs of needed help and failing to step in, an example may be an aging parent who is having difficulty managing (or is denying) incontinent issues and the home has an odor of urine. No one really wants to have a conversation with mom or dad about incontinence, however necessary it is. But it must be done. (Have your sister do it!! That's supposed to be a joke.)

Out of respect for aging parents and in keeping with a biblical upbringing, often adult children are hesitant to step up and step in, when necessary, to gently intervene when situations call for it. As a result, children will often turn a blind eye when parents repeatedly make unwise financial decisions, continue to live in unsafe conditions, willingly neglect medical treatment, or knowingly engage in risky daily activities.

Everyone makes poor decisions from time to time. We might eat too much, drive too fast, refuse to see a doctor when needed, fail to exercise adequately—the list of poor choices is endless. The accounting of our own sins makes it even more difficult to sit in judgment of our parents' poor choices.

Nevertheless, adult children still have a responsibility to ensure their aging parents are safe, well-cared for, and loved. Neglecting to respectfully—not in a patronizing way—address issues that may harm them dishonors parents.

Over the years, I have encountered many such situations where children have allowed parents to live in unsafe conditions. Some aging parents have lived in upstairs apartments, yet never stepped foot outside their home because they were unable to manage the stairs. (I shudder to think what would have happened in the event of a fire.) Some aging parents have repeatedly caused minor fender-benders with their car because of poor eyesight or the inability to gauge distance. I have smelled the stench of rotting flesh because of lack of medical care. I have been in homes infested with vermin, watching cockroaches crawling up and down the walls. And I have been in the homes of hoarders who didn't even have a path between rooms but were required to walk on top of debris covering every inch of the floor. These were all circumstances where children not only refused to intervene, but in some cases, participated in poor decisions and living conditions.

Just like the driving scenario previously mentioned, these situations can be hard to manage for everyone involved. No one wants to yank their parents from their home, take away the keys, or drag someone to the doctor against their will. And while the laws allow individuals to make decisions affecting their lives if they are deemed competent, governmental agencies, such as the Department of Health and Senior Services, have the authority to investigate and intervene if poor decisions create situations that are unhealthy or unsafe. I am not talking about matters of self-determination, such as poor dietary choices but rather life-safety decisions and situations such as remaining in housing that is condemnable or a disoriented individual who wanders unsupervised.

There is a fine line between allowing aging parents to be autonomous and honorably ensuring that they are safe, well-cared for, loved, and not abandoned. So how do you lovingly and respectfully intervene?

Riding in like gangbusters is probably not a good approach. Cockles are likely to rise, heels will probably be dug in, and adult children will probably find themselves in a stand-off with their parents.

A softer approach usually works best. Asking questions such as, "Are you ever concerned when [this] happens?' or "What does the doctor say about [this]?" or "Did you notice [this], which is somewhat alarming?" Another way of addressing issues is to offer help in a way that is not controlling, but still helpful. "Mom, I am concerned when you stand on a chair to change the lightbulb. It would give me peace of mind if you would let me know when that needs to be done so I could help you with that" or "I know you like to mow the lawn, but it would be a blessing for me if you would allow me to do that every week, Dad. Please do not take away my blessing."

It is important to maintain a sense of trust with parents. Keeping them involved in what is going on and being honest about what concerns you regarding their care and well-being is paramount. In addition, never lie to them because you cannot establish or maintain a trusting relationship built on lies. Proverbs 12:22 says, "Lying lips are an abomination to the Lord. But those who deal truthfully are His delight." And Proverbs 15:1 reminds us that "A soft answer turns away wrath, but a harsh word stirs up anger." Both of these proverbs are true, especially in our relationships with our parents.

Honestly, it is a sticky-wicket knowing at what point aging parents can, and should, be allowed to make autonomous decisions and at what point adult children should, or must, intervene for the sake of safety and well-being. Either way, a sense of integrity and respect must be afforded aging parents through open communication that, in addition to concern, expresses love and honor.

The second way adult children can obey parents and still dishonor them is with their attitudes. Even when children obey their parents, provide proper care, and ensure their safety, if those tasks are performed begrudgingly or with a disrespectful attitude, rather than with love, dignity, and compassion, the ensuing result is dishonor. For example, agreeing to help Mom clean her house weekly can be an honoring way to exhibit love and care. But if, during the course of cleaning, a barrage of complaints is made regarding the time it is taking, or the messes Mom has created throughout the week ensues, the act that was originally designed to honor and help Mom has now become one of dishonor.

Life can get hectic and demanding—and so can aging parents. Adult children are tugged in many directions and sometimes parents do not seem to understand all the pressures and stressors that are often part of everyday life. Physically and emotionally, adult children, who are often providing financial and other assistance to their own children, have little energy to fulfill the biblical command to honor their aging parents. Nevertheless, just as parents have a responsibility to faithfully meet the needs of minor children regardless of career obligations or time constraints, the command to biblically honor aging parents also stands despite life stressors that arise.

Granted, aging parents may not fully understand the level of busyness their children are engaged in. They may even become so focused on their own needs and wants that they lose the ability to differentiate and prioritize those tasks that require immediate attention versus those that can be put on a to-do list for later. Because the ability to recognize the difference between needs and wants is often misconstrued, that will be a topic of discussion coming up in the next chapter.

Nevertheless, God's command to honor parents is not conditional. He doesn't say, "Honor your parents only if they aren't too demanding," or "Show kindness to your parents only if they show kindness to you (or your spouse)," or "Respect your parents only if they respect your time, space, privacy." What God said was, "Honor your parents." Sometimes, that can be a tall order.

CHAPTER THREE
When I Am Honoring My Parents, Could I Be Dishonoring Myself?

Well-meaning adult children who are caregivers committed to honoring their parents often allow themselves to be consumed with responsibilities of care. Sometimes they believe they are the only ones who can provide proper care. Maybe they have an inability to tell parents "no" or perhaps they are trying to rid themselves of guilt for dishonorable behavior in the past. There could be any number of other reasons or excuses that may result in a mindset whereby adult children over rationalize the self-importance of the care they provide their parents. Even though the intentions are good, and the adult child makes every effort to provide superior care, when caregiving responsibilities become overwhelming, there is a risk that the adult child will inadvertently dishonor themselves or other family members. It is important that adult children honor their parents, but it is equally important that they do not dishonor themselves in the process.

Dishonoring oneself can involve one or multiple aspects of life. According to Dr. Richard Johnson, author of the book, *Caregiving from Your Spiritual Strengths*, individuals who dishonor themselves may neglect their own physical or spiritual needs, fail to fund their own basic needs, give up contact with friends and family, and/or psychologically abuse themselves, such as using self-talk that is harmful, shaming, or abusing. If, for example, a parent falls while in the care of the adult child, despite it being no fault of the child, the child may allow guilt to consume them resulting in a self-talk that tells them they are a lousy caregiver. Dishonoring oneself also can occur if exhaustion has set in due to lack of sleep because the aging parent needs round-the-clock supervision due to wandering or other physical care needs, yet the child caregiver refuses to allow a sibling or other respite worker to temporarily step in to spot them.

It can become easy to allow caregiving responsibilities to overwhelm or consume one's life. Not only do adult children desire to be faithful and honoring to their parents, but often they have their own children and grandchildren that need time and attention. Sometimes, unintentionally—or unknowingly—obstacles and situations are created that complicate the caregiving role and cause adult children to dishonor themselves. Usually, this happens when caregivers and children try "too hard." The desire to do their best to provide exemplary care, meet all needs and wants, and give their complete attention overrides personal needs and becomes destructive and dishonoring to the adult child.

To keep a balance between biblically honoring parents by meeting their care needs and not allowing those intentions to dominate or dishonor other aspects of life, in his book, *How to Honor Your Aging Parents: Fundamental Principles of Caregiving,* Dr. Johnson suggests three ways adult children can manage their caregiving responsibilities:

1. Be cautious of creating unnecessary dependence
2. Watch for overcommitment
3. Understand the real needs of parents and be able to distinguish these from the wants they may request

Considering and following Dr. Johnson's recommendations will facilitate caregiving responsibilities, but more importantly, it will encourage healthy interactions between the adult child and their aging parent.

Be Cautious of Creating Unnecessary Dependence

What does unnecessary dependence look like? It could be doing tasks for aging parents that they could do for themselves, and then the parents come to expect the task will always be done for them. It could be isolating parents so that the adult child becomes the parents' sole social, emotional, spiritual, and physical support. It could be shielding aging parents from normal risks and responsibilities of living by creating a sense of fear if they go outside or answer the phone. It could even be something as simple as accompanying a parent to a doctor's appointment and then speaking to the doctor about the parent as though the parent is not in the room. Often physicians are guilty of initiating this type of interaction, so it is important that the adult child redirect the conversation to include their parent. That could be done simply by saying something such as, "What do you think about what the doctor just said, Mom?" or "What other concerns do you have that you would like to discuss with the doctor while we are here today, Dad?"

Most often, the actions related to the creation of unnecessary dependence are not done maliciously. In fact, they are usually done with the best of intentions, as adult children try to be helpful. I have found myself guilty of this, and I remember how emotionally devastated I was when I realized how detrimentally crippling—both physically and emotionally—my actions had been. To take away a person's independence, the control they have over their life—well, it is the same as stripping them of their dignity, their self-worth, their reason for being. It is a terrible thing. That is not to say there are not instances where frailties or other conditions may warrant or necessitate assistance, but this assistance must done with care and compassion—with a feather of kindness, not a bulldozer of determination.

Watch for Over-Commitment

Sometimes the relationship between the aging parent and the adult child is off-balance. Maybe the adult child overcommits because of a personal need to be needed rather than fulfilling an actual need the parent has. Perhaps the overcommitment is rooted in guilt for a strained past relationship. Maybe the adult child desires to be seen as a "good" son or daughter by others—particularly their parents with whom they may be jockeying for an elevated position among siblings; or maybe it is simply based on a realization that the days are short. When adult children overcommit themselves, eventually resentment seeps in and other relationships suffer.

As a long-term care administrator, some of the most difficult family members to work with were adult children who had been providing full-time care to a parent. Mind you, these children were well-intentioned and were striving to honor their parent. Yet, frequently, caregiving children become consumed with performing tasks they think are necessary for their parent's well-being yet actually do little to improve their quality of life. To complicate the matter, it is common for them to believe no one else can, or will, properly care for the parent like they do, so it is difficult to allow others to step in to help. The caregiving child may complain about no one else helping them care for the parent, but in the same breath, they may not allow or ask for help. If help is offered and given, they may control or criticize the way it is performed.

Having personally experienced full-time caregiving, I can appreciate, and relate to, the concerns of the caregiving child. It is hard to step away for even several hours, much less several days. I have found myself writing out pages of detailed instructions so the respite caregiver would know and be able to perform the daily tasks with as little disruption to the routine as possible. Even as I am writing out these instructions, I realize I am not writing them for the respite worker or for the one I care for; I am writing the instructions out for my benefit, to make me feel better—less guilty—about leaving.

Keeping up that unreasonable level of care becomes exhausting and overwhelming, and when the caregiving children can no longer keep up with the high standards of care they have set for themselves, resentment can set in. Resentment does not replace love, but it does manifest itself in short tempers and sharp tongues, which is usually spewed out on other family members as well as the parent. The caregiving child becomes the martyr and believes no one can understand or appreciate all they have done or endured.

Exhausted, the caregiving children may eventually seek help from professional caregivers, such as home health care services or long-term care placement. It is possible that other family members may even insist on it because the caregiving child has dishonored themselves and the other family members for too long. Even so, if the parent comes to live in long-term care, often the caregiving child's overinvolvement does not stop. Whereas children providing full-time care can devote their full-time attention to the parent, that is an unreasonable expectation in long-term care where there are numerous others also needing attention. Nevertheless, that expectation is frequently carried over into the long-term care setting. Well-intentioned children may even try to re-create the living arrangements the parent had at their house, demanding that the long-term care staff perform trivial tasks to maintain that scenario. And when they come to visit, if those standards have not been followed, Katy, bar the door! In other words, the long-term care staff can expect a heap of trouble.

Although not uncommon (I have seen this happen repeatedly), the above situation is probably an extreme example of adult children becoming overly committed and overly involved in parental care. However, even lesser situations of overcommitment can result in resentment, guilt, and anger—even mistreatment—directed at the aging parent and other family members. No adult child committed to the care of their parent desires or expects the emotional distance that occurs when they dishonor themselves or others. For these reasons, it is necessary to achieve and maintain a balance of honor, commitment, and independence.

Where Needs End and Wants Begin

There are certain basic needs everyone has: food and water, shelter, safety, sleep—and I would add love and affirmation. To properly honor your aging parent, there are additional needs they have that, although not considered basic, should be met. Those include intimacy and a sense of belonging, socialization, having a purpose and meaning in life, and respect.

Oftentimes, aging parents as well as their adult children get confounded and misguided as to where "needs" end and "wants" begin. This is a complex topic that will be discussed at length in the following chapter.

In the meantime, suffice it to say, attempting to accommodate every wish and whim of aging parents, as well-meaning as it might seem, is often unreasonable and can easily lead to situations that dishonor oneself.

Questions to Consider

1. Have you ever been in a situation where you wanted to honor or fulfill a request of your parent while at the same time knowing that this would not be in their best interest?

An example of this might be an aging parent instructing their children never to sell the family farm or an otherwise significant piece of property and desiring their promise not to do so. Because future finances and care needs cannot be predicted, that is a promise that may not be able to be kept, particularly if care needs become so great they require staggering amounts of funding. Long-term care is very expensive, and it is common that the sale of property (or a lien being placed against the property) becomes necessary, by law, to pay for it.

As honorable and well-intentioned as the original promise may have been, what should a child do if they agreed to such an assurance and can no longer keep that promise? If it is impossible to keep a promise, the child has no option but to admit their mistake in making the oath, explain the reason the promise cannot be kept, and ask for forgiveness. The parent may express anger, disappointment, sadness, or—best case scenario—understanding and forgiveness.

Sometimes, promises are made in haste without consideration for potential long-term ramifications. Before agreeing to a pledge, it is wise to slow down the process to think about how it might play out in the future. So, when asked to make a promise, an appropriate response could be, "Although I would like to agree to that promise, Mom, I cannot. I will do my best to honor your wishes. However, I am not certain I will be able to fulfill the promise in the future and I would not wish to dishonor you by making an oath I cannot keep."

2. Have you ever found yourself in a situation that seemed as if honoring your aging parent would mean dishonoring yourself and/or your family?

Family traditions—long-standing ones as well as the making of new ones—could easily be an example of a situation where honoring an aging parent could also dishonor other family members. As children mature and start their own families, it is common for them to want to start their own traditions. Sometimes these new customs conflict with time-honored ones, both in the way the traditions are handled as well as the timing of when they occur. Adult children (the middle generation, also known as the Sandwich Generation), are often caught in the middle, wanting to please and honor their aging parents by preserving previously established customs, and yet be part of the new traditions their children are forming.

If an aging parent has not learned to roll with life's punches or to adapt to change, they may look at new ideas with a wary eye, finding these unfamiliar ways of doing things threatening, a means of excluding them, or an otherwise offense to the old order. Attempting to restore a sense of balance, the aging parent may use manipulation by becoming angry and belligerent, verbally attacking family members, or crying. If they become desperate to restore a sense of control and order, they may even threaten harm to themselves or others.

A less dramatic example could simply be the adult child being torn between spending time with the aging parent and other family members who also need, deserve, and expect time. Perhaps the aging parent has an unrealistic time expectation. If the adult child does not adequately fulfill that expectation, it is not uncommon for the aging parent to find reasons why the adult child must spend time with them. Those reasons could include "illness," something needs to be fixed, paperwork needs to be done, or transportation needs to be provided for a trivial matter. The possibilities are only limited by the aging parents' imagination.

In this instance, one way to respectfully honor parents' need for attention yet preserve time for self and others could include identifying and establishing time limitations at the outset. Explaining that there is an hour available twice a week, for example, that the parent can decide how it will be used establishes boundaries as well as gives the parents a sense of control in the ways their needs and wants can be met. They can choose to spend the adult child's time visiting, going for a drive, fixing a leaky faucet, mowing the lawn, paying bills, cleaning the bathroom, or whatever else the parent needs or wants done.

When an elderly aunt, whose children did not live close by, became a widow, I offered to step in to assist her with business affairs as well as providing company in her sense of loss and loneliness. Because I had other care responsibilities, we agreed that I would visit once a week for two hours. In preparation for my visit, my aunt would make a list of the things she wanted to accomplish that day. Sometimes, before I left, we even planned out the next week's visit: who we would call, where we would go, what we would do. She knew, if she truly needed me, she could contact me on other days during the week, but she was good about respecting the boundaries that we had agreed upon, which made our planned visits very enjoyable and productive.

> 3. Have you ever been in a situation when you wished to, or thought it best to say "no" to your aging parent, yet you "gave in?"

Granting wants and wishes is not a bad thing. Doing so can create enjoyment and fun memories, and it can strengthen bonds. Yet, sometimes, adult children can be asked to do things that are not necessarily wise or even honoring. These requests can put adult children in a quandary. Do I do what Dad asked of me, even though it may create a problem in the future? Or, do I say "no" and create a problem today?

Years ago, I had an older friend who asked me to do something that I knew was a bad idea. Not only did the request comprise my values, I realized it could also potentially have a negative impact on many others for whom I was responsible. Because I was sympathetic to her cause, I reluctantly agreed to my friend's request to allow a behavior to occur that I knew was not honorable—and I immediately regretted it. In the end, I had to confess my unwise decision and apologize to the others it impacted. Several lessons were learned by that experience, including how difficult it is to say "no" to someone you care about and the humbling aftermath of consequences for failing to do the right thing despite well-meaning intentions. In this situation, I dishonored both myself and many others.

Not only do we have difficulty saying "no" to those we love, but many times, those we love also expect us to acquiesce to their requests and demands despite the risk we take of dishonoring ourselves or others. The good news is that, generally, we know, and can even predict in some instances, when dishonor is occurring or will occur. It is easy to become entangled in situations that are dishonoring. However, we also have a responsibility to change those situations. This can be accomplished by recognizing and managing needs and wants, by accepting help when needed, and by learning to say "no."

CHAPTER FOUR
Dealing with Difficult Behaviors of Aging Parents

There is a debate—at least in my mind—of whether personality changes with age. Some people assert that, particularly in the case of dementia, older adults experience a personality change. I have always thought it would be an interesting study to determine if that is, in fact, true or if this apparent change is actually a result of what is in our core being, now surfacing at a time when our social controls have weakened.

Social controls regulate our public behavior. For example, belching aloud in public is not acceptable, but when in our own home, with no one to offend, we may enjoy a good, loud burp. Maybe we use a refined language in public whereas at home, the air may sizzle with words not meant for others to hear. When we are younger, our social controls keep us in check. As we age, however, those social controls may be comprised, either due to dementia or simply a lack of restraint. I remember when my mother turned 70. She said, "I am now 70 years old, and I have earned the right to say whatever I want." And she did!

Over the years, I have had numerous adult children

express to me their horror at the language their mother or father has started using. Previously, these children had never heard their parent utter a single obscenity, and now Mom is cursing like a sailor or Dad is making lewd remarks. I have thought a lot about the shock these children experienced. To shield my own children from such a surprise, I have told them, "If, when I get older, I start to use words you have never heard me say, do not be alarmed. I have been thinking them all along!" So, are these seemingly new behaviors and language really new, or have they been suppressed by public expectations and social controls for years and are now set free?

What I have seen over the years is that, rather than older adults experiencing a personality *change*, what often happens is that they experience a personality *concentration*. For example, if an individual is kind and sweet and giving as a young person, they will become even more so—more kind, more sweet, and more giving—as they age. If a person has spent a lifetime being bitter and angry, by the time they reach old age, they will be even more bitter and more angry. If someone has gotten through life manipulating others into doing what they need or want, by the time they hit old age, they will be a professional manipulator.

Manipulation is probably the most difficult behavior to contend with as it manifests itself in many forms. Manipulators may use guilt, anger, crying, or threats of harm to self or others. Although it is impossible to address every possible situation, in this chapter, general ways to honor aging parents while being aware of manipulative behaviors—and guarding against those behaviors—will be explored.

Distinguishing Needs from Wants

Often it is difficult and uncomfortable for adult children to tell parents *no* when parents instruct them to fulfill expectations that are not needs, especially if these desires put the child in a bad position—with siblings, spouses, and/or children. The dilemma can become even more conflicted when the edict just doesn't seem like the right or God-honoring thing to do. In His command to honor parents, God does not expect His children to do anything that is against His will, to do anything that will dishonor Him, or to do anything that will dishonor any of His children.

In God's command to honor parents, nowhere does He say adult children must grant the fulfillment of both needs and wants. However, sometimes "wants" are couched in terminology making them sound as though they are "needs." This can make it difficult to distinguish between the two. It is important to understand the difference between the needs of parents that must be met to honor them opposed to wants that are desired but can be lived without. However, even when adult children recognize the difference between the needs and wants of parents, *knowing* and *doing* are two different aspects of caregiving and communicating with aging parents.

Understanding the difference between needs and wants is the beginning of creating an awareness of manipulative behavior. Often the words "need" and "want" are used interchangeably, leading the listener to lose sight of what is really being expressed. For example, Mom might say, "I need you to tell your sister to visit me more often" or she might say, "I need you to help me set up my medications every week." The first statement is not a need. Mom is trying to manipulate one child into engaging another in a situation bound for conflict. The second statement is probably a need, especially if Mom is having difficulty properly taking her medications.

An aspect of honoring parents is the expectation that their basic needs be met, including their need for comfort and support. Those aspects of honor are not debatable. At the same time, it is also nice when children can grant some of their parents' wants and wishes. However, in some cases, those wants and wishes are not in the parents' (or the child's) best interest.

Identifying and Dealing with Manipulative Behaviors

Manipulative behaviors are fairly easy to define. They include behaviors such as lying, blaming, giving the silent treatment, threatening, criticizing, and withholding important information. Another form of manipulation is gaslighting. A simple definition of gaslighting would call it a strategy used to gain or maintain control over someone by creating confusion whereby the person being gaslit believes they are to blame for circumstances that go wrong. Over time, they may believe ideas or situations that are not true and may even believe they are losing their mind.

Although manipulative behaviors are easy to define, they are not always easily spotted by the one who is the target. However, the targeted individual is usually aware of an uncomfortable or bad feeling when the manipulation is occurring. That unpleasant feeling is the clue.

Everyone uses manipulation to some degree, usually to achieve a desired result such as garner cooperation or change behavior. Perhaps the manipulation is in the form of a compliment: "You performed [that task] very well. Now, could I get you to help me with [this task]?" Maybe it is in the form of a bribe: "If you will do [this], then I will give you [this]. Sometimes the manipulator uses guilt and shame: "You were raised better than to do [this], and when you do [this] it makes the entire family look bad." Some people will resort to threats, such as yelling in anger, crying, or even talking of self-harm or harm to others.

Manipulation is used because it works! Parents don't just suddenly start manipulating others when they reach old age. They have likely been using this coping mechanism to get what they want for a lifetime. Not only has it worked over their lifetime, but they have also honed and perfected it over the years. And their children have been conditioned to respond in ways that perpetuate the cycle. For example, Mom may intentionally compare one child's devotion to her with another's, causing strife between the two children and a constant need to win Mom's approval. Or, without regard for the different gifts God has bestowed on his children, Dad may chastise one child for the inability to fix something.

Breaking out of the cycle can be tough. No one wants to see their mother cry. No one wants to be yelled at by their father. Even as adults, a child may think, "If Mom harmed herself, I could never forgive myself for not just doing what she wanted."

So, how can adult children respectfully break a lifelong cycle of unhealthy behavior? The first task will be to determine if the request—or in some cases, the demand—is a need or a want. If it is a need, then it must be done. If it is a want, then there is some discretion as to whether it must be granted. In any case, there is nothing dishonoring about adult children helping their parent restate the request in a way that does not perpetuate unhealthy manipulation.

A few years ago, there was a woman who would come to my office every day to complain about something. Every day was a new complaint that she wanted me to fix. It got to the point where I dreaded seeing her walk through the door. Eventually, it dawned on me what was happening: she was lonely and needed a reason to talk to me. I finally said to her one day, "You know, you can come to see me anytime you want, even if you don't have a problem." "*Really?*" "Yes, Ma'am." After that, she never presented me with a problem again. She just came to visit, and both of our lives got better.

Sometimes, we must look beyond the words and behaviors to determine what has triggered the need for manipulation. Is Mom's guilt trip due to a need for a myriad of home repairs done today, with even more on the list for tomorrow? Or does she just miss you and is lonely for your company? Is Dad just fearful of losing his independence when he accusingly yells at someone for moving or taking the car keys (when he was the one who misplaced them)?

Most of the time, emotions drive behaviors. Adult children cannot change the behaviors of their parents. However, by acknowledging and validating emotions and fears, the behaviors will change. In other words, if adult children start communicating differently, the aging parent will begin responding differently. Years ago, I was presented with a visual example of this: if you take a bowl full of marbles and remove one from inside the center, the remaining marbles will shift as a result. That is a good illustration of how, when adult children make a positive change, it will trigger a positive response from their aging parent.

Blaming, Accusing, Whining, and Complaining

The four behaviors of blaming, accusing, whining, and complaining are common characteristics of early dementia and are particularly difficult to manage. If parents do not have a history of being complainers or whiners, it may come as a surprise when Mom or Dad starts complaining about situations that never bothered them before. If they have been life-long complainers, adult children can expect the complaints to magnify. This chapter—this book— will not be addressing dementia and how to care for parents with dementia in depth. However, because these behaviors fall under the category of being difficult to contend with, it is fitting that an explanation be given with general suggestions of how to honor parents when this situation arises.

For purposes of definition, the terms "dementia," "disorientation," and "Alzheimer's Disease" are often used interchangeably, and although they contain many of the same characteristics, there are differences that make them distinctly unique. Briefly, "dementia" is a broad term used to encompass behaviors such as forgetfulness, confusion, and even falling. Dementia is progressive and debilitating, and it is usually attributable to specific diseases such as Alzheimer's Disease or Parkinson's Disease. "Disorientation," or confusion, is an altered mental state causing an inability to think clearly; it can be a temporary condition brought on by medications or medical conditions, such as urinary tract infections, in older adults. "Alzheimer's Disease" is a specific disease, usually diagnosed by process of elimination after other medical testing has revealed no other medical reason for symptoms of dementia. It is only definitively diagnosed upon autopsy.

Individuals with dementia are generally thought of as being forgetful or disoriented. In advanced cases, they may not know where they are, what the day or time is, or even what the names of family members are. However, there are also other characteristics that may not be recognized as signs or symptoms attributable to the beginning stages of dementia.

For example, Mom may be oriented to person, place, and time, but she may say something that is very odd and out of character. Maybe she expresses some paranoia that was not present in the past. Perhaps Mom accuses trusted family members of theft. During a visit with Mom, she may say, "Your sister was here yesterday, and now my best underwear is missing. We wear the same size and I think she stole them." Dad may say the neighbors are poisoning him or spying on him. Mom may complain about unreasonable things. Dad may blame someone or something for changes or losses he is experiencing. Rather than acknowledging nighttime urinary incontinence, he may say, "There is a leak in the roof; that is why my bed is wet every morning." Even in the early stages of dementia, hallucinations and delusions may occur, and Mom may believe that a man is under the bed or there are small children who need care. Some of these behaviors are ways aging parents deal with loss, which will be discussed in the next chapter.

When parents in the early stages of dementia are still oriented to person, place, and time, adult children may believe they can rationally communicate with them to offset the behaviors of blaming, accusing, whining, and complaining associated with loss. However, the opposite is true as reason has been replaced by fear. Like a life preserver, aging parents are desperately clinging to a sense of control and independence because they recognize that their losses are jeopardizing those precious things. Each loss they experience, both large and small, is cumulatively building, threatening to snatch away those two greatest forms of self-identity. When control and independence are lost, life feels like it is spiraling out of control.

Yet, trying to convince aging parents of reason and reality—that they are wrong—is futile. Strategically proving the neighbors are not spying on or stealing from them or arranging a face-to-face confrontation with a caregiver to mediate and refute accusations of theft, generally will not achieve the desired results. I speak from experience: In my early years in long-term care, when I was just getting my feet wet, Mrs. Sullivan relentlessly accused a nurse aide of having an affair with her husband every time she gave him a bath. I thought if I could just mediate a conversation between Mrs. Sullivan and the caregiver to discuss the matter, Mrs. Sullivan would come to realize that the aide was simply performing the necessary caregiving tasks that her husband required and that there was nothing untoward occurring between them during the bathing process. Because I focused on the facts of the matter rather than Mrs. Sullivan's insecurities and sense of loss, the meeting was a disaster. Lesson learned: I never conducted a meeting like that again.

As with Mrs. Sullivan, aging parents do not respond well to being corrected or confronted with reality. Therefore, arguing with them only makes it worse, and the adult child will never win the argument. Children cannot fix their parents or alter the losses associated with aging. In addition, aging parents who are behaving in ways that are unreasonable, or irrational do not respond to insight or therapies such as behavior modification. They do not want to be analyzed; they need to be understood and accepted.

Besides attempting to correct parents' faulty thinking, there are two other approaches children will often resort to in desperation: agreeing with the parents' faulty thinking and irrational belief or using distraction. Think for a moment about the consequences of agreeing with the irrational belief. By agreeing with faulty thinking two things occur. First, strong emotions such as fear, anger, and distrust are unnecessarily being perpetuated. Second, the parent has been lied to. Imagine believing the neighbors are spying on you and your family member, whom you trust, acknowledges or verifies your belief. That validation does little to alleviate the situation, but rather intensifies the emotions. Lying, under any circumstances, is not acceptable. Not only is it dishonoring to parents, but it also violates the commandment given in Exodus 20:16, which says, "You shall not bear false witness against your neighbor." In the simplest terms, Christians are commanded not to lie. Thus, lying to parents not only dishonors parents, but it dishonors God.

On the other hand, as already mentioned, telling parents the truth—correcting them—doesn't work either. Refuting the accusation of spying not only creates distrust between the parent and the child, but the parent may then believe the child is also spying on them or is otherwise in cahoots with the neighbors.

The use of distraction serves to only ignore the issue or emotion aging parents are experiencing rather than allowing them to talk about it. Often adult children are afraid to talk about unpleasant or uncomfortable issues, believing if it is discussed openly, it will only serve to make the parent think more about it. It is much the same concept as talking with someone who is feared may be contemplating suicide; if it is talked about with that person, or if the person is asked about it, then the fear exists that the conversation may cause the individual to think even more about it. However, talking about emotions does not make them worse. Rather, validating emotions allows people to feel heard and understood.

So, you can't lie, you can't tell the truth, and you can't use distraction. Quite a conundrum, isn't it? Yet, there is an honorable way to communicate with parents who display these behaviors that does not involve the sin of lying, the upset of correcting the parent, or the mistake of ignoring of strong emotions. Rather than *telling* the parent what to think or feel, ask questions. In her book, *The Validation Breakthrough: Simple Techniques for Communicating with People with "Alzheimer's-Type Dementia,* Naomi Feil, suggests acting like a reporter—asking who, what, when, where, how, and what if questions—allows the parent to express thoughts and emotions in a nonjudgmental arena. (Did you notice "why" was not in the list of questions to ask? "Why" questions require logical thinking, and in this case, the parent is usually not thinking logically, making "why" questions both irrelevant and frustrating.)

So, using the scenario of "spying neighbors," the line of questioning could go something like this:

"It's really upsetting to think your neighbors are spying on you, isn't it, Dad? When does it generally happen? Who do you think is involved? What do you think they are trying to learn about you? What is the worst thing about it? Does it ever *not* happen? What if it stopped happening?"

These questions do not acknowledge truth in the accusation, nor do they attempt to correct faulty thinking. Rather, by allowing the parent time to process and answer the questions, the adult child explores and validates strong emotions. At the same time, they express interest in and acceptance of parents in a loving and honorable way.

This approach also involves listening to the meaning and emotion behind the words and talking about those. For example, do you hear fear in his voice when he talks about the neighbors? Do you hear anger? Distrust of those around him? What would cause Dad to suddenly distrust the neighbors? Has he had his trust broken in the past? To formulate proper questions, using empathy, imagine what Dad might be feeling and why. An appropriate response might be, "It sounds like you don't trust your neighbors. It is important to be able to trust people, and it must be a terrible feeling to live close to people you don't trust. Have you ever had a situation where you couldn't trust people before? How did you handle that situation? Is it possible to approach this problem in a similar way?"

If the adult child is familiar with the parent's history, they may even be able to provide encouraging conversation that reduces anxiety and stress for the parent. For example, using the same scenario of mistrusting the neighbors, the adult child might say, "I remember a time when the neighbor boy borrowed a tool from your shed without asking. You didn't appreciate what he did, but you handled him with mercy. How do you think you could handle this current situation in a similar manner?"

Remembering that adult children cannot fix their aging parent, this line of nonjudgmental questioning encourages parents to draw upon experiences from their past to aid them in solving present-day problems.

Other Difficult Behaviors

Many adult children report embarrassment by their aging parents' rude or critical remarks to unsuspecting or undeserving others. These comments are usually made in public settings or during phone calls and cast a sense of humiliation upon children and other family members. Like manipulation, perhaps the aging parent makes harsh comments because others will acquiesce to their demands, even if it is just to put an end to the encounter.

On the other hand, it is possible that this behavior represents underlying fears and experiences that the aging parent is having difficulty dealing with. Take, for example, a mother who calls the post office daily to ream out her mail carrier because he is late with her mail. If she has nothing to do but wait for the mail, perhaps the mail represents a relief from loneliness. Maybe she is hoping for correspondence from family or friends. What if she has always been conscientious about paying her bills on time and she fears being sent to "collections" because the bill arrived late? Maybe a phone call, even an unpleasant one, simply gives her someone to talk to.

In the event of unwarranted or unnecessary criticisms, if done respectfully, there is nothing wrong with expressing hurt at criticisms. Saying something such as, "It really hurt my feelings, Mom, when you criticized me in front of others," or "I realize you care about me, and I need to lose weight, but when you point that out every time we are together, it does little to motivate me."

When the parent is angry at the adult child, it can be emotionally devastating for the child. As hard as it is, the adult child may need to depersonalize hurtful remarks. Depersonalizing does not mean denying the accusation or cause of the anger but rather acknowledges it by saying something such as "I am sorry you are hurt at the thought I may have acted against you. I can understand how you would become angry. I love you very much and would never wish to hurt you." A response such as that does not admit guilt and does not patronize the parent. Instead, it acknowledges the hurt and affirms the love the child has for the parent. On the other hand, if the adult child did commit a sin against the parent and anger and disappointment are warranted, then the child should acknowledge the sin and ask forgiveness.

Tools for Disarming Difficult Behaviors

It is good to have a quiver full of tools to draw from when faced with difficult behaviors from aging parents. These techniques do not necessarily need to be complex, but it is helpful if they are varied as one arrow may not disarm every behavior every time. In addition, although the techniques described in this section are not complicated and do not require a college education, they may call for practice as they are probably not the first response of adult children dealing with difficult behaviors from aging parents. In fact, usually, the first response of adult children is one of emotion, often based on fear, frustration, or some other factor that obstructs effectively communicating with aging parents. Adult children need to recognize their emotions and know how to keep them in check. A good mental picture is to visualize placing your fear, anger, sadness, etc. in the closet and shutting the door, at least for the moment, while dealing with the situation at hand. Once the crisis or frustration is over, you can take your emotions back out of the closet and process them.

I recognize this can be a difficult challenge. I did not always handle situations with my mother correctly. I remember the day she hitchhiked from her house to my office. I was planning to pick her up in just a few minutes, and I was not late. However, she was anxious to get to me and was no longer driving. So, she took it upon herself to arrange for her own transportation. When I learned what she had done, I nearly had a come-apart. I could just picture her walking alongside the road with her thumb out, my mind going wild, even seeing her with her pants leg hiked up trying to get someone to stop. She could not tell me the name of the man who had picked her up and delivered her to my office. "Well, I know him," she said. Well, I didn't! I chastised her for not waiting for me. I let my fear of "what could have been" overwhelm me, and I took it out on my mother.

At that point, the reality was, Mom was safe (except maybe from me). If I had kept my emotions in check, I would have dealt with the situation much differently. "You were very eager to get to see me this morning, Mom. Were you afraid I had forgotten you? I was very frightened to learn that a man I didn't know picked you up and brought you to my office. I hope, in the future, you will trust that I will pick you up as we plan." This type of approach would have acknowledged Mom's anxiety and even rationale for her poor decision-making. It would have conveyed to her my love and concern for her well-being, and would have, hopefully, set the groundwork for future situations involving transportation and trust. Once I had calmly talked with Mom and was later by myself, then I could have taken my emotion of fear out of the closet and had a private come-apart.

Although specific tools and techniques will be discussed to assist with disarming difficult behavior of adult parents, sometimes the approach can be something as simple as knowing what verbiage pushes the button of the aging parent. For example, with my father, I knew the word was "odor." That is a word he would use, and I was aware he found the idea of having an odor to be highly undesirable. So, in the last months of his life, he started refusing to take a shower. When my brother, who was his primary caregiver, told me of Dad's need to bathe and his refusal to do so, I simply asked Dad, "You don't want to have an odor, do you?" He replied, "No." Then he got out of bed and took a shower.

Using a word or phrase that resonates with the aging parent is a very simple tactic that I, truthfully, just stumbled upon. But it worked. Although several other, more tried techniques will be explored in this section, the potential options of tools are vast, limited by what works and doesn't work.

Asking Questions

As previously mentioned, asking questions is a way to circumvent situations that are precarious. This is true regardless of whether aging parents have dementia. Rather than engaging in direct confrontation, a gentler, often more disarming approach can lead, rather than pull aging parents in the proper direction. In addition, asking the right questions will frequently result in the parent drawing their own, more appropriate conclusion to a situation. This asking-rather-than-telling approach is much more palatable.

For example, in the event of a demanding parent, the adult child might ask questions such as: "It's important that [this task] be completed in a timely manner. When would you like it to be accomplished? Who do you think should be involved in the process? How long do you expect it to take? What happens if it is not completed on time?" These questions assure the parents that they are heard and are being taken seriously because they are being asked for their input about the process. The questions also set the stage for the possibility that the task may not be completed as expected. By asking questions, the adult child can also get a sense of what emotions the parent may be experiencing, and by using empathy, they can identify—by looking beyond the words—what is driving the comments and behaviors. This process helps the adult child verbalize for the parent the message that is behind the behavior.

Asking questions can also be a way of taking the monkey off the adult child's back by allowing the aging parent to confess difficult situations they are facing without the adult child being the bad guy who brings it to light. For example, if there is a concern about nutrition or cooking safety, the adult child might start a conversation about fixing an upcoming holiday meal and say, "That's a lot of work for you, isn't it, Mom?" Most likely, Mom will agree. Follow-up questions could be, "Do you find the day-to-day cooking burdensome?" "In what ways is meal preparation problematic?" "How could it be made easier for you?" "Is there something I could do to help take the burden off of you?" Rather than accusing Mom of not eating properly or of not feeding Dad appropriately—and insinuating she is failing or less than adequate—asking questions may allow her to feel safe enough to admit her difficulties and have an honest conversation.

On the other hand, especially in cases of advanced dementia, asking and expecting to receive logical responses is often unrealistic and requires a different approach. My youngest brother loved our mother very much and, despite her progressing dementia, he would regularly call her at the nursing facility just to chat. One day, he contacted me for advice because he was experiencing frustration at his inability to make sense of both Mom's responses to his questions as well as the questions she was trying to ask him. My advice to him was simple: Stop asking questions. Not only could Mom not think logically, she also could not remember the appropriate answers. So, instead of asking questions in this case, I suggested that my brother approach their visits differently. Rather than expecting Mom to remember how to answer his questions, he could do the remembering for her.

For example, instead of asking, "Do you remember when you would have dinner parties with the neighbors?," he could change the question to a statement and say, "I remember when you would invite our neighbors over for big dinner parties. You were a great cook and a wonderful hostess, Mom. Everyone always enjoyed those parties. And more importantly, Mom, you taught me to love *my* neighbors." This approach not only removed the pressure on Mom to remember, but it brought back sweet memories and validated the positive impact she had on both our neighbors as well as her children.

Mirroring

Mirroring—or matching movements, sounds, and emotions—could be a good way to start a conversation with a parent who is angry. For example, if Dad is obviously upset and angry about a situation, the adult child, using the same tone of voice and expression, may say something such as, "That really made you angry, didn't it, Dad? It would have made me angry too!" Then, acting like a reporter, the adult child could ask questions: "What aspect of that situation was the most upsetting? Has anything like this ever happened before? What do you think is the best way to handle it? How do you think God would have you address it?" Telling Dad not to be mad, ignoring his anger, or even smiling when talking to him will not reduce the strong emotion of his anger.

These same types of questions can be substituted for any emotion, including fear, sadness or grief, distrust, disappointment, or depression. Telling aging parents how they should feel does not honor them. Likewise, forcing aging parents to suppress emotions by suggesting that they should get over it, or worse, completely dismissing the emotion without acknowledging it only results in a resurfacing of the emotion or situation later. Asking questions that explore and validate strong feelings and emotions result in parents experiencing a sense of relief as well as respect and honor from their children who express a genuine interest in them.

Mirroring emotions and behaviors can be done even with parents who have advanced dementia, and it can be an effective tool to facilitate communication on a level adult children may have not previously considered. In its most progressed state, dementia often strips individuals of the ability to communicate using intelligible language. Perhaps dictionary words are replaced with non-dictionary words that simply feel good to say. Some clinicians may refer to it as "word salad" because word sounds become mixed up or jumbled. In addition, sometimes dementia causes individuals to revert to communicating using pre-language sounds such as clucking or clicking.

Mirroring those unintelligible words and pre-language sounds may seem disrespectfully mocking. However, if done properly and with compassion, mirroring those sounds is a basic way of communicating. It is not necessary that adult children understand the actual meaning of the words and sounds. Instead, it is most helpful to listen for the general meaning. For example, if Dad sounded frustrated and said something such as, "That dad-gum flabbergaster…," a proper response might be, "That dad-gum flabbergaster is really irritating you, isn't it? Is the flabbergaster not working right?" It doesn't matter what a flabbergaster is, the important thing is respectfully communicating by meeting Dad where he is.

Even in my mother's most advanced stage of dementia, I would talk to her as though she understood every word I said – and maybe she did, who knows. As part of my normal jabbering talk, I often would wink or make a clicking sound with my tongue for emphasis. It was interesting to watch as Mom would mirror *me*. If I winked at her, she would wink back. If I made a clicking sound, she repeated the sound. Although she could not speak intelligible words, she was still communicating with me.

Taking a Time Out

When an encounter with an aging parent is not going well, sometimes the most honoring thing for an adult child to do in the event of conflict is to respectfully walk away to allow for a cooling off period. "I can see, Dad, that we are not getting anywhere today discussing this matter. I love you and will stop by tomorrow after we have both had time to think over possible solutions." Such a response is not defamatory or disrespectful. It acknowledges the conflict, and it expresses love and honor. It also gives time for both parties to reflect on ways to resolve issues that may not be possible in the heat of the moment.

This time out period is not to be used as an act of stonewalling. Although the topic of conversation may be unpleasant or cause major disagreement, neither party should refuse to talk it over. Likewise, this time out period should not be used to ignore or dismiss the issue, but rather to pause for a period to calm down and think clearly. Ignoring an issue does not make it go away. Failure to acknowledge the elephant in the room does not mean the elephant is not there. The issue remains as an open wound until it is resolved.

If a time out is called, a time frame should be

established for when the conversation will reconvene. Once the time to meet again is agreed upon, the adult child needs to fulfill that time commitment to maintain a sense of trust. Trust is paramount in maintaining an honorable relationship.

What if a solution or compromise to an issue cannot be found or is not reached? Sometimes, aging parents may dig in their heels and refuse to budge (and adult children can be just as stubborn). If the parent insists on making an unwise or unsafe choice, and has not been declared incompetent, the adult child should allow the aging parent to make the decision. For example, Mom may defy the recommendations of her doctor by refusing to take medication or follow a restrictive diet, thereby putting her health in serious jeopardy. However, the child is not required to condone or participate in it. To maintain honor and respect, the child could simply say something such as, "Mom, I respect your right to make this choice. However, it seems an unhealthy decision, and I love you too much to participate in it."

Managing difficult behaviors exhibited by aging parents can be uncomfortable and trying. Nevertheless, it is important that adult children manage those behaviors in a way that is honoring—even if the behaviors seem dishonorable. It is not the role of the child to judge the parent. That position belongs to God. The adult child only has the responsibility to love, accept, and honor their parent.

CHAPTER FIVE
Understanding Losses and How They May Affect My Aging Parents

When I was in my early years of ministry at The Baptist Home in Ironton, Missouri, a long-term care facility, under the tutelage of Joy Goodwin, I remember her saying it was important that the staff learn more than caring for the physical and psychosocial needs of the residents. In addition to the important skills of caregiving, she asserted, it was important also that they discover how to age well themselves by learning to adapt to losses in life rather than becoming stuck and unable to move on.

Joy described it as learning to play multiple keys on the piano of life, not just getting stuck playing a single note. In her wisdom, Joy was saying that it is difficult to make the beautiful music of life that God intends us to enjoy without adapting to the changes and opportunities for growth that He places in our lives. We need to be able to roll with life's punches and to offer the forgiveness that God commands of us in Scriptures such as Matthew 6:14 which says, "For if you forgive men their trespasses, your heavenly Father will also forgive you," and Ephesians 4:32 where Paul tells us, "Be kind to one another, tenderhearted, forgiving one another, even as God in Christ forgave you."

The losses we experience in life come in many forms and are not defined just in terms of death or health concerns. Losses involve life changes such as children moving away, a change in or termination of a job, retirement, relocating to another community, or even simple things like needing to find a new doctor or getting a new boss. The older we become, the faster losses come and the harder they hit. I am now at an age when losses are arriving at a rapid rate. As far as successful adaptation to loss and graceful aging is concerned, I am not sure how well I am faring. However, I am trying to employ the skills of flexibility and forgiveness that Joy worked to instill in me. I am so thankful for the loving way she taught me to care for the emotional needs of the elderly. I have used those skills throughout my career, and most importantly, with my mother who had dementia.

Showing Sensitivity to Loss

For adult children to properly honor their parents, it is important that they be sensitive to the changes created by loss that are often associated with age. I have heard it said that the two most tumultuous times in life—the two times that require adaptation to the most changes—are during adolescence and old age. The process of aging presents a dichotomy whereby experiences over a lifespan open the door creating vast differences in individuals, yet this same aging process also results in a shrinking of one's world. Material items often lose their value, possessions are reduced to a minimum either by choice or necessity, and physical losses may limit the ability to leave the home or participate in family events. Where once there was a full house of family and possessions, today the aging parent's sphere may be reduced to a single room either in a family member's home or a nursing facility.

With age, the value of relationships replaces the value and importance of material items. The loss of relationships, especially through death, impresses their importance and value. Where once there were many relationships with family and friends, the majority of those may be compromised or lost because of geography, societal changes, estrangement, or even death. The loss of relationships, regardless of cause, is often much harder to accept than the loss of belongings. Many times, however, material belongings come to represent important relationships from the past, and those items are held tightly. For example, my mother cherished a framed print of flowers. It was not a particularly attractive print. It was a cheap picture in an inexpensive metal frame. However, my mother told me she treasured this print because it was the last birthday gift her mother gave to her before dementia ravished her mind, creating an inability to remember birthdays or special holidays and events.

Frequently, though, family members do not recognize the importance of these seemingly trivial items. Without realization or consideration, or the proper recognition for what or who they represent, precious memories are often discarded without thought. Until her death, the cheap floral print my mother cherished hung on the wall near her bed, even once she entered a nursing facility.

I am a purveyor of old and unique items. Some of the items in my home hold sentimental value due to their history within our family. Some of the items have value due to their rarity. And some of the items caught my eye due to their uniqueness but are just worthless junk. I have children who are minimalists. They have no appreciation for the collectors-of-dust around my house and give little thought or assign little to no value even to those items of historical family sentiment. On the other hand, I also have a daughter who has an eye for the unusual, has her own dust collection, and is interested in and appreciates learning the history of my items. I have tried to share with her a catalog of items: those which are part of our family history, those which hold some monetary value, and those which are unique pieces of junk. As I age, I recognize that my dust collection is mostly just "stuff," and although I enjoy it now, it will not be difficult for me to part with most of it—when the time comes…most of it.

Knowing the difference between items aging parents consider valuable—particularly items of sentimental value—and items that are just stuff is very important. Properly honoring aging parents includes a sensitivity to the importance of seemingly unimportant items. As parents age and their world shrinks, taking the time to allow parents to sort through, touch, and share stories of their items permits them to remember stories of previous and precious life experiences and the past relationships associated with items. Showing an interest in stories also provides adult children with an opportunity to learn precious family history that could be on the brink of disappearing.

Besides material items, the list of potential losses that aging parents might experience is long. It is not only long, but these losses can appear in multiples requiring parents to juggle the onslaught at a faster and faster pace as life goes on. Imagine trying to juggle three balls, then suddenly two more balls are added into the mix. And then two more. Is it any wonder aging parents become overwhelmed with the changes and losses they are experiencing? Is it any wonder that they hunker down and seemingly give up the juggle? It can feel like there are too many balls of loss to contend with.

Consider what it might be like to lose your eyesight and your ability to drive at the same time. Imagine that your spouse dies and combined with that loss you lose the income needed to live independently. Picture having your memory fail along with your bladder. With age, losses come faster and faster and start piling up at a rate that may test the faith of parents. When their world starts falling apart, often adult children are called upon to pick up the pieces. These pieces could take the form of providing emotional support along with transportation, additional financial assistance, even picking up incontinence products at the store.

Being empathetic to the losses of aging parents is a valuable approach and is not as difficult to achieve as one might imagine. For example, adult children with aging parents have, most likely, started to experience their own losses associated with aging. Children may have moved out, either to college or to start their own families. Retirement may be looming, creating a loss of role and purpose and necessitating a redefinition of identity. Physical changes have started to occur, such as menopause. I've heard it said that once you hit the age of 50, the "check engine" light starts to come on, as chronic conditions begin to challenge activities that were once taken for granted. (If you don't believe me, try skipping. Not only is it more difficult to coordinate those movements due to age, but various orifices must be tightly clenched, especially when jumping, sneezing, or laughing so as not to create embarrassing accidents.)

By recognizing the emotions and challenges presented by their own life losses and changes, adult children can naturally imagine the emotions parents are experiencing. Coupling this empathy with attention to what is valued—relationships and belief systems as well as material items—adult children can be better prepared to honor their aging parents by helping them cope with the onslaught of losses.

Coping with Loss

The way aging parents manage or cope with losses can be fairly predictable because, usually, people resort to coping skills they have used all their lives. Some people rely strongly on their faith and accept the losses as God's will. That approach does not mean they do not grieve, but it does mean they do not get stuck in their grief. They have often learned to roll with life's punches and to adapt to losses. Comments indicating a healthy way of dealing with loss and adapting to the resultant changes might be, "I can no longer go to church, but I can still pray for others and watch a religious service on TV" or "I can't fix my meals any longer, but I am willing to accept Meals on Wheels." On the other hand, maybe aging parents believe God is punishing them for their sin or lack of faith. This perspective may be indicated through statements such as, "If I had attended church this week, then God would not have punished me by making me sick, causing me to fall, or letting my cat die."

Other aging parents may deny their losses and the difficulties those losses create. For example, they may say, "There is nothing wrong with my hearing! You mumble!" or "There is no reason I can't drive! I have never even had a speeding ticket! I am a good driver, and my eyes are fine, regardless of what that police officer told you." Mom may not say anything but denies her inability to control her bladder by placing her wet undergarments over the heat register or lamp shade to dry, creating a noticeable odor in the home.

Rather than denying their losses, maybe the older parent blames someone or something—sometimes even God—for their losses. This perspective may be revealed through statements like, "If you would come to see me more often, then I wouldn't be falling," "If that doctor would have prescribed me the right eye drops, then my eyesight would not be failing," or "That pole was put in a dumb place. Otherwise, I wouldn't have hit it with the car!"

Another coping method is to whine, complain, or act like a martyr, saying things such as, "No one appreciates how hard I try. All they ever do is criticize me for leaving the stove on, and it wasn't even my fault." Maybe they accuse others—even trusted family members—of things like theft when they can't remember where they put something. "Your sister was here the other day and stole my favorite lipstick. I know she did it because it's been missing ever since she was here."

If accusations were made against someone such as another family member or a trusted friend, what would you think? Would you believe the accusation? Typically, if the item missing is of no value, such as a tube of lipstick, underwear, or costume jewelry, the accusation is likely not true. Instead, the parent has probably misplaced the item, and rather than take responsibility for forgetting where they placed it, they blame others of theft. Interestingly, when the item is eventually located, rather than admit they had misplaced it, often the aging parent will assert that the "thief" returned the item. Rarely will aging parents acknowledge their misconception of what really happened (that they misplaced the item and forgot where they put it).

On the other hand, if the missing item has value, such as a diamond ring, cash, or an expensive heirloom, before confronting the accused, it is probably best if adult children respectfully ask the parent if they could help the parent search for the missing item. Frequently, the item has been tucked away for safe keeping or has even been stashed away in plain sight but is being overlooked. Many times, the missing item of value can be located without causing hurt feelings or unnecessary conflict within the family.

When aging parents use poor or unreasonable coping skills in response to loss, such as blaming or accusing, it is best that adult children do not respond by taking the accusations personally or expressing anger toward the parent. In addition, shaming or correcting the parent is not the answer either. At the same time, adult children are not required to, and should not, acquiesce to whatever the aging parent wants particularly if it is unhealthy, sinful, or futile. Sometimes, adult children choose to distance themselves from their aging parents to avoid conflict, however, that is rarely a good response either.

Remember the "war" we are striving to win? The one to maintain a positive, healthy, loving, and honoring relationship with our aging parents? This is another time when we must choose our battles. Do not be baited into an argument or allow hurt feelings to jeopardize your relationship due to Mom or Dad's harsh, accusatory words.

Losses don't just affect aging parents; losses also impact other family members, particularly adult children. Having been used to witnessing the strength of parents, who always knew what to do, how to handle situations, how to adapt to life changes and loss, and had the right words of advice, it hurts the children to witness physical and mental frailties in parents. When the steps of aging parents' falter, when their eyes dim, when their memory fails, or when their thinking becomes twisted, it grieves adult children to realize their parents—maybe, their heroes—are no longer the invincible stalwarts they were viewed to be. Upon seeing the struggles parents face in old age—when faced with their frailties—it is painful. It is truly watching heroes falter.

Often, the ways adult children cope with the faltering of aging parents—either physically or mentally—are by using similar coping skills they learned at their parents' knee, such as accepting on faith, blaming, denying, and accusing. Adult children may also try to fix or correct their aging parents when they say or do something that is not right. For example, adult children may think if they tell their parents loudly enough, or sternly enough, they will understand and do better. That approach does not yield the desired or intended results. Usually, it serves to drive a wedge between the adult child and the parent. No one appreciates being corrected, so understandably, aging parents will, most likely, resent being corrected by their adult children.

In the case of aging parents with dementia, disputing an accusation of theft by others will destroy (or further jeopardize) trust, as often the parent will turn on the adult child, claiming they are in cahoots with the thief. Arguing, even with the intention of helping the parent see reason, is dishonoring and rarely helpful.

My mother called me one day in a dither saying, "The plumber was here yesterday, and he stole the TV remote." Now, the reality is, the plumber would have no use for her remote control. I did not agree that the remote had been stolen, but rather I simply asked, "Would it be okay if I came by to help you look for it?" She agreed. When I got there, the remote was on the arm of the couch, where it always stayed. I did not chastise her or shame her, but said, "It can be frightening when a stranger is in your home and you do not know if you can trust them, isn't it?" "Yes, it is!"

Not only do parents resent attempts by their children to fix or correct them (which often takes the form of, or results in, arguing), adult children are also not capable of fixing their parents. To fix aging parents would require the ability to change or alter the losses the parent has experienced related to aging, and that is not possible.

As adult children care for aging parents, it is important to keep in mind the barrage of the losses being experienced, the grief they feel, and the coping skills they are employing as they try to adapt to their ever-changing world. Adult children need to be cognizant of how they react—both to the responses and reactions of their aging parent and to their own emotions and how those are expressed. Arguing, shaming, or rebuking does not show honor to aging parents.

Just as aging parents experience grief over their losses, adult children may also share that grief as they witness the losses of their parents. However, children cannot remain paralyzed in their grief. Just as parental loss requires adjustment by the parent, it also often requires adult children to adapt, physically to the increasing needs of parents as well as emotionally to the change in mental capabilities. Perhaps assistance is now needed with transportation to the doctor because the aging parent can no longer see to drive. Perhaps adult children must do the grocery shopping because the parent has difficulty walking or is at risk of falling. Maybe adult children must provide financial support because a spouse has died, resulting in loss of monthly income. Perhaps children must check on parents daily to make sure they are safe or arrange for services that will allow them to stay in their home. If feasible, children may need to bring parents into their home or consider placement in long-term care. Parental losses often trickle down to adult children, and the command to honor parents may transform into an aspect of honor and care that adult children had not had to undertake or consider previously.

CONCLUSION

Despite the seemingly straightforward Scriptural command to honor parents, respectful and honorable care of aging parents can be very complex. Often, it is the day-to-day struggles facing adult children that cause a build-up of simple frustrations that can be overwhelming and result in situations that are regrettable and unintended.

Understanding the difference between honoring and obeying provides adult children with a foundation for biblically relating to their aging parents. When that is coupled with being able to differentiate between needs and wants, children can better prioritize their caregiving responsibilities.

Even so, telling parents "no," even with this understanding, can cause a feeling of uneasiness – almost as though a sin is being committed. However, done respectfully, there are times when saying "no" is the God-honoring thing to do.

The behaviors of aging parents can be difficult to manage. In the case of behaviors that are intentionally manipulative or self-serving, it may feel awkward or wrong to challenge your aging parent. On the other hand, if your parent has a loss of cognitive functioning, such as is often the result of dementia, they cannot necessarily be held responsible for their behaviors and the frustration it causes family members.

My father used to become so irritated with my mother when he could not get her to understand and cooperate with what he wanted her to do. For example, he would give her a simple command such as, "Go over there," When she did not go "over there," he would say it again, more sternly. Listening to this interaction hurt me, and I finally said to him, "Mom does not understand where 'over there' is. She does not understand what you want her to do because of her dementia. It would be better if you took her by the hand and gently led her to where you wanted her to go." On another occasion, he shared his frustration with me at Mom's behavior. To elicit empathy, I asked him to remember how stately and beautiful and intelligent Mom used to be. Then I said, "She would still be that way now if she could…but she can't. She would do better, act more appropriately, and understand what you wanted her to do if she could…but she can't. She needs you to love her and accept her as she is."

Adult children experience the same frustration and the same hurt. It grieves children to watch their heroes falter, knowing they are helpless to change or fix the losses of aging their parents are facing. A preacher once told me, "The problems of this life are temporal and temporary." How true. Despite losses parents experience, regardless of day-to-day frustrations and irritations caused by the difficult behaviors parents exhibit, in spite of physical and emotional exhaustion due to the needs and demands of caregiving, one day it will be no more. One day, "they that wait upon the LORD shall renew their strength; they shall mount up with wings as eagles; they shall run, and not be weary; and they shall walk, and not faint."

> *"Do not cast me off in the time of old age;*
> *Do not forsake me when my strength fails."*
>
> Psalm 71:9

BIBLICAL REFERENCES
New King James Version

Introduction

- Ephesians 6:4 – And you, fathers, do not provoke your children to wrath, but bring them up in the training and admonition of the Lord.

- Proverbs 29:17 – Correct your son, and he will give you rest; yes, he will give delight to your soul.

- Colossians 3:21 – Fathers, do not provoke your children, lest they become discouraged.

Chapter One

- Exodus 20:12 – Honor your father and mother, that your days may be long upon the land which the Lord your God is giving you.

- 2 Corinthians 9:6-7 – But this I say: He who sows sparingly will also reap sparingly, and he who sows bountifully will also reap bountifully. So let each one give as he purposes in his heart, not grudgingly or of necessity; for God loves a cheerful giver.

- Deuteronomy 5:16 – Honor your father and your mother, as the Lord your God has commanded you, that your days may be long, and that it may be well with you in the land which the Lord your God is giving you.

- Genesis 1:27 – So God created man in His own image; in the image of God He created him; male and female He created them.

- Psalm 139:13-14 – For You formed my inward parts;

  You covered me in my mother's womb.

  I will praise You, for I am fearfully and wonderfully made.

- Psalm 139:16 – Your eyes saw my substance being yet unformed.

  And in Your book they all were written,

  The days fashioned for me,

  When as yet there were none of them.

- Isaiah 46:4 – Even to your old age, I am He,

  And even to gray hairs I will carry you!

- Matthew 6:26 – Look at the birds of the air, for they neither sow nor reap nor gather into barns; yet your heavenly Father feeds them. Are you not of more value than they?

- Matthew 16:26 – For what profit is it to a man if he gains the whole world, and loses his own soul? Or what will a man give in exchange for his soul?

- John 15:13 – Greater love has no one than this,

than to lay down one's life for his friends.

Chapter Two

- Ruth 1:6-17 - Then she [Naomi] arose with her daughters-in-law [Orpah and Ruth] that she might return from the country of Moab, for she had heard in the country of Moab that the Lord had visited His people by giving them bread. ⁷Therefore she went out from the place where she was, and her two daughters-in-law with her; and they went on the way to return to the land of Judah. ⁸And Naomi said to her two daughters-in-law, "Go, return each to her mother's house. The Lord deal kindly with you, as you have dealt with the dead and with me. ⁹The Lord grant that you may find rest, each in the house of her husband."

   So she kissed them, and they lifted up their voices and wept. ¹⁰And they said to her, "Surely we will return with you to your people."

   ¹¹But Naomi said, "Turn back, my daughters; why will you go with me? Are there still sons in my womb, that they may be your husbands? ¹²Turn back, my daughters, go—for I am too old to have a husband. If I should say I have hope, if I should have a husband tonight and should also bear sons, ¹³would you wait for them till they were grown? Would you restrain yourselves from having husbands? No, my daughters; for it grieves me very much for your sakes that the hand of the Lord has gone out against me!" ¹⁴Then they lifted up

their voices and wept again; and Orpah kissed her mother-in-law, but Ruth clung to her.

¹⁵And she said, "Look, your sister-in-law has gone back to her people and to her gods; return after your sister-in-law."

¹⁶But Ruth said: "Entreat me not to leave you, Or to turn back from following after you; For wherever you go, I will go; And wherever you lodge, I will lodge; Your people shall be my people, And your God, my God. ¹⁷Where you die, I will die, And there will I be buried. The Lord do so to me, and more also, If anything but death parts you and me."

- Luke 15:11-32 - ¹¹Then He [Jesus] said: "A certain man had two sons. ¹²And the younger of them said to his father, 'Father, give me the portion of goods that falls to me.' So he divided to them his livelihood. ¹³And not many days after, the younger son gathered all together, journeyed to a far country, and there wasted his possessions with prodigal living. ¹⁴But when he had spent all, there arose a severe famine in that land, and he began to be in want. ¹⁵Then he went and joined himself to a citizen of that country, and he sent him into his fields to feed swine. ¹⁶And he would gladly have filled his stomach with the pods that the swine ate, and no one gave him anything.

¹⁷"But when he came to himself, he said, 'How many of my father's hired servants have bread

enough and to spare, and I perish with hunger! ¹⁸I will arise and go to my father, and will say to him, "Father, I have sinned against heaven and before you, ¹⁹and I am no longer worthy to be called your son. Make me like one of your hired servants."'

²⁰"And he arose and came to his father. But when he was still a great way off, his father saw him and had compassion, and ran and fell on his neck and kissed him. ²¹And the son said to him, 'Father, I have sinned against heaven and in your sight, and am no longer worthy to be called your son.'

²²"But the father said to his servants, 'Bring out the best robe and put it on him, and put a ring on his hand and sandals on his feet. ²³And bring the fatted calf here and kill it, and let us eat and be merry; ²⁴for this my son was dead and is alive again; he was lost and is found.' And they began to be merry.

²⁵"Now his older son was in the field. And as he came and drew near to the house, he heard music and dancing. ²⁶So he called one of the servants and asked what these things meant. ²⁷And he said to him, 'Your brother has come, and because he has received him safe and sound, your father has killed the fatted calf.'

²⁸"But he was angry and would not go in. Therefore his father came out and pleaded with him. ²⁹So he answered and said to his father, 'Lo, these many years I have been serving you; I never

transgressed your commandment at any time; and yet you never gave me a young goat, that I might make merry with my friends. ³⁰But as soon as this son of yours came, who has devoured your livelihood with harlots, you killed the fatted calf for him.'

³¹"And he said to him, 'Son, you are always with me, and all that I have is yours. ³²It was right that we should make merry and be glad, for your brother was dead and is alive again, and was lost and is found.'"

- Proverbs 12:22 – Lying lips are an abomination to the Lord,

But those who deal truthfully are His delight.

- Proverbs 15:1 – A soft answer turns away wrath,

but a harsh word stirs up anger.

Chapter Four

- Exodus 20:16 – You shall not bear false witness against your neighbor.

Chapter Five

- Matthew 6:14 – For if you forgive men their trespasses, your heavenly Father will also forgive you.

- Ephesians 4:32 – And be kind to one another, tenderhearted, forgiving one another, even as God in Christ forgave you.

Conclusion

- Isaiah 40:31 – But those who wait upon the Lord

    Shall renew their strength;

    They shall mount up with wings like eagles,

    They shall run, and not be weary,

    They shall walk, and not faint.

- Psalm 71:9 – Do not cast me off in the time of old age;

    Do not forsake me when my strength fails.

REFERENCES

Feil, Naomi. *The Validation Breakthrough: Simple Techniques for Communicating with People with "Alzheimer's-Type Dementia."* 2nd ed. Baltimore: Health Professions Press, 2002.

Johnson, Richard P. *Caring for Aging Parents: Straight Answers That Help You Serve Their Needs Without Ignoring Your Own.* St. Louis, MO: Concordia Publishing House, 1995.

Johnson, Richard P. *How to Honor Your Aging Parents: Fundamental Principles of Caregiving.* Liguori, MO: Liguori Publications, 1999.

Johnson, Richard P. *Caregiving from Your Spiritual Strengths: The Ten Fundamental Principles for Optimal Success (The Spiritual Strengths Healing Plan).* n.p., 2013.

Owsley, Don. "What Does the Bible Mean to Honor Your Parents?" Relavate Counseling Ministry. September 17, 2020. https://www.relavate.org/discipline/2020/9/17/what-does-the-bible-mean-to-honor-your-parents.

Owsley, Don. Pastoral Counselor. Virtual interview by author, Arcadia, MO, March 4, 2022.

Snider, Sherri A. *Equipping Adult Children from Arcadia Valley, Missouri Churches in a Biblically Informed Process to Honor Aging Parents.* DMin diss., Midwestern Baptist Theological Seminary, 2022.

Trimm, Charlie. "Honor Your Parents: A Command for Adults." *Journal of the Evangelical Theological Society* 60, no. 2 (2017): 247-63.

Additional Resources

Alzheimer's Association, www.alz.org.

Area Agency on Aging. To find the AAA nearest you, go to www.eldercare.acl.gov/public/about/agency/network.

Hourglass Care, LLC. Hourglasscare@facebook; www.HourglassCare.com.

The Validation Institute, www.thevalidationinstitute.com.

ABOUT THE AUTHOR

Sherri Snider has felt a calling to work with older adults her entire life and served 38 years in long-term care, 26 of those as a nursing home administrator. She has been a certified Validation therapist for 35 years and has conducted numerous training seminars for various audiences across Missouri. Beginning in 2015, she began traveling abroad to train elder care leaders, social workers, pastors, university students, and mental health professionals in the United States commonwealth of Puerto Rico and in the countries of Belarus, Ukraine, Moldova, El Salvador, Guatemala, and Nicaragua.

Snider holds a Doctor of Ministry from Midwestern Baptist Theological Seminary and a Master of Social Work from Saint Louis University. In addition, Dr. Snider is a licensed clinical social worker and a licensed nursing home administrator.

Dr. Snider is also author of a children's book, "Pippa Learns About Gran's Dementia," designed to lead children (as well as adults) through the progression of dementia and offer ways to fulfill God's command to honor parents and grandparents by addressing fears, questions, and adjustments to life changes. It also provides simple instructions on how to engage grandparents in life review, which validates the importance of their lives in ways that even children can understand. Using biblical teachings and principles, the book is designed to help children, ages 4-12, learn to respectfully honor grandparents, understand simple ways to relate to those with dementia, and know with confidence that, even if memory fades, love remains.

In addition to *"No, Mom! Can I Tell My Aging Parents 'No' and Still Honor Them?"* Dr. Snider will be addressing other issues of biblically-honoring care that face adult children, including dementia care and end-of-life care, in future books.

She can be contacted for speaking events or individual support at Hourglass Care, LLC on Facebook, at Hourglasscare.com, or at sherri.snider@gmail.com.

www.ingramcontent.com/pod-product-compliance
Lightning Source LLC
Chambersburg PA
CBHW070520030426
42337CB00016B/2039